An
Organization Development
Approach to
Management Development

An Organization Development Approach to Management Development

GLENN H. VARNEY
Bowling Green State University

 ADDISON-WESLEY PUBLISHING COMPANY
Reading, Massachusetts
Menlo Park, California
London · Amsterdam
Don Mills, Ontario · Sydney

ISBN 0-201-07982-8
BCDEFGHIJ-DO-7987

Preface

After many years of designing, conducting, and justifying management development programs, I came to the conclusion that classroom instruction, seminars, and packaged programs designed to develop managers do not, in reality, contribute to the personal development of managers to the extent to which I had thought. With considerable curiosity, I studied why some men moved up in organizations while others didn't. What I found was that successful managers had experienced unique opportunities in their careers which allowed them to develop their own individual talents. In many of the success cases I found little or no exposure to formal management development.

This led me to the conclusion that management development as we have conceived it in many organizations is nonproductive —and in some cases probably counterproductive to the development of managerial talent.

This book takes a new look at how managers develop. The reader is encouraged to test the ideas and concepts presented here in terms of the processes and practices now used to develop managers in their own organizations.

Credit for writing Chapter 3—and for preparing Fig. 9.2— goes to Dr. Frank Friedlander (Case Western Reserve University). My personal thanks are offered to all those who have endured me during the writing of this book.

Bowling Green, Ohio   G.H.V.
January 1976

Contents

1/How Managers Develop – A New Look

Management development in a large number of organizations tends to be relatively ineffective—and in some cases a counter-productive process which, in fact, may be doing an immeasurable amount of damage to the organization. Oftentimes management development (MD) programs tend to be based on the notion that "If it's education—it has to be good." Usually in such cases, the investment in MD produces results which are not measured and often turn out to be the opposite of those intended.

The stark reality of this conclusion presents itself when you study closely many MD programs. Although our conclusions are oversimplified here, if they were not at least partially true, then how else can we explain the fact that an individual with one set of personality and intelligence variables may be a failure in one situation, while in another organization under another set of conditions he or she may turn out to be a success?

Let's take an example of a young man who, on graduation, entered a management training program for a large manufacturing company. The training program was highly structured, following organizational values and norms. It was impersonal in terms of the individual's goals, while the program goals tended to be rather ambiguous. The subject in this case felt frustrated, uncertain, and highly dependent on the organization. At the conclusion of the program, he was assigned to a department on the basis of very high evaluations from the program coordinator. After six months on the job, he was dismissed for "incompetency" and lack of "technical skills." He then went to another company where he was able to design his own career development plan. His own personal values and beliefs were taken into consideration in the development planning. It was clear in which direction he could and wanted to move. He felt in step with the company and the program, and he felt that his efforts contributed to his own as well as the company's success. Today he is a key executive in this organization.

You may react to this example by saying that it was due to the man himself, not the organization. The man was young and inexperienced; he didn't know what he wanted, and so on. But when the example is examined closely, the obvious difference is that the new environment was more conducive to this man's personal growth and development.

If we are objective in our analysis, we must ask ourselves some basic questions relative to our well-established and somewhat traditional approaches to management development:

1. Why does a highly organized management development (MD) program fail for some people, while succeeding for others?

2. What are the critical differences between a successful MD effort and an unsuccessful MD effort?

3. What are the appropriate learning processes which need to be applied to a specific person within a specific organizational context?

4. What structural variables and factors tend to stimulate the growth of a manager within an organization?

The purpose in writing this book is to first of all examine how MD has been practiced in the traditional and more structured sense up to now. Second, we will pose a challenge to you to examine MD in a different way—one which we believe to be a more "natural" approach. And third, we will look at some relevant concepts in organization development as they relate to MD, and how these concepts can be used to develop an appropriate set of organizational and human conditions for optimal human growth and the development of individuals interested in moving up in the organization.

DIFFERENCES AND SIMILARITIES BETWEEN MD AND OD

Clearly, both MD and organization development (OD) are strategies for change. That is, when an organization sets out to train managers so they can function effectively in management positions to which they may be assigned in the future, it is attempting to change these managers so their behavior will fit the desired behavior pattern for optimal results at that future level in their careers. Both management development and organization development, as indicated by their names, imply a systematic way of changing the functioning of an individual and, therefore, the functioning—and ultimately the effectiveness —of the organization.

A useful comparison of MD and OD was made by Dr. Warner Burke, who concluded that, "Many organizations have been involved in both management development as well as OD during the past several years." Many organizations claim that they are conducting *organization* development when, in fact, what they are doing is conducting *management* development. Still others are conducting organization development activities under the name of management development. Warner Burke compares OD with MD along a number of dimensions, as summarized in Fig. 1.1.

Fig. 1.1 A comparison of organization development and management development

Category	Organization development	Management development
Reasons for use	Need to improve overall organizational effectiveness	Need to improve overall effectiveness of manager
	Tough problems to be solved; typical examples:	Managers do not know company policy or philosophy
	–inter-unit conflict –confusion with recent management change –loss of effectiveness due to inefficient organizational structure –lack of teamwork	Managers are void in certain skills Managers seem to be unable to act decisively
Typical Goals	To increase the effectiveness of the organization by: –creating a sense of "ownership" of organization objectives throughout the work force –planning and implementing changes more systematically –facilitating more systematic problem-solving on the job	To teach company values and philosophy To provide practice in management skills which lead to improved organizational effectiveness To increase ability to plan, coordinate, measure, and control efforts of company units
	To reduce wasted energy and effort by creating conditions under which conflict among people is managed openly rather than handled indirectly or unilaterally	To gain a better understanding of how the company functions to accomplish its goals

Category	Organization development	Management development
	To improve the quality of decisions by establishing conditions under which decisions are made on the basis of competence rather than organizational role or status To integrate the organization's objectives with individuals' goals by developing a reward system which supports achievement of the organization's mission as well as individual efforts toward personal development and achievement	
Interventions for producing change	Education and problem-solving is on-the-job; learning while problem-solving and solving problems while learning Following a diagnosis, utilization of one or more of the following techniques: –team building –training programs –intergroup confrontations –data feedback –techno-structural interventions —change in organizational structure —job enrichment —change in physical environment (social architecture)	Send manager to some educational program Job rotation of managers Specialized training "packages" Courses and/or conferences Involved in counseling Reading books and articles
Time Frame	Prolonged	Short, intense
Staff Requirements	Diagnostician Catalyst/Facilitator Consultant/Helper Knowledge and skill in the dynamics of planned change Experience in the laboratory method of learning	Teacher/Trainer Program Manager Designer of training programs Knowledge in the processes of human learning

Although Burke suggests that the goal of MD is to improve the overall effectiveness of a manager, as contrasted with the goal of OD—which is the improvement of the overall organization—we would argue that in both OD and MD organizational change does indeed take place. The difference is as follows: MD induces organizational change as the organization stimulates behavioral change in the individual (the change may or may not be to the behavior which was intended). As the individual conforms to the organization's requirements, the real change in his or her behavior is usually slight—and may sometimes be inconsistent with or intolerable to the purposes of the organization. OD processes, on the other hand, are designed to set up the conditions and provide the opportunities for individuals to develop along unique lines, thus stimulating organizational change through their own behavior modification. Management development attempts to change the individual in the direction set by the organization, while organization development allows the individual to grow and develop—and thereby change the organization.

In one MD effort with which we are familiar, a group of high-level managers in a large company went through a program of three MD sessions, each lasting one week. The program was structured along typical MD lines. It was offsite from the company and was based on the "latest behavioral science" concepts involving motivation, group dynamics, and all the current "topics." At the end of the first week the participants were highly enthusiastic and ready to apply their new learning to the organization. On their return for Phase II, several weeks later, the managers appeared somewhat disgruntled and concerned about their ability to use their newfound ideas and admitted that they couldn't see how those ideas would apply to the real world. After some discussion, the core of the problem boiled down to the fact that the organization (and specifically the managers for whom these men worked) would not allow them the opportunity to use the new knowledge; in fact, in some cases application was openly discouraged and mocked.

The concern of the participants mounted, and finally they decided to confront the issue directly by inviting the president and several officers of the company to a "rap session" with them.

The chief executive and his subordinate officers were, therefore, invited to dinner. Following a somewhat subdued meal they were cornered by the group and asked what they were going to do to make it possible for the program's participants to try out their ideas. The next morning the personnel vice-president received a letter from the president stating that training which resulted in this type of confrontation was to be eliminated, or altered in such a way that it did not "disturb the organization."

We argue that this is not an altogether untypical problem in many MD efforts, and that a contrasting OD approach to manager development would follow a different approach. Such an approach would first examine the nature of the tasks to be accomplished by the organization; then it would consider the nature of the "people component" in the organization. From this evaluation would come a set of organizational structures designed to optimize the development of all people in order to maximize accomplishment of the tasks which the organization is also attempting to achieve. The basic structure affecting human growth and development would, therefore, be designed around the tasks of people—as contrasted with a MD approach, in which people are trained and developed to fit the basic structure existing within the organization. An MD approach is a rather static and oftentimes incongruent system in relation to human beings, whereas the OD approach is a more flexible and more congruent system. This basic notion will be the underlying proposition for this book.

FOCUS AND ORGANIZATION OF THE BOOK

At the outset we want to be clear that our objective is to stimulate individual growth within an organization in order to fill the increasing need for people to assume higher levels of responsibility in their organizations.

As you read on, you may find it difficult at times to think about developing managers within the broader framework of the entire organization. We are, in fact, more accustomed to focusing on classroom approaches to learning than on the total environment for learning.

Chapters 2 and 3 will provide a historical framework and a closer look at our basic proposition, as well as setting forth a model around which the book is written. Chapters 4 through 9 will examine specific components of an OD approach to developing managers and will provide a set of operational approaches which you can use to examine your own organization. We will conclude the book with an attempt to integrate our ideas into an overall approach so that the reader may take the ideas back to his or her organization and apply them. Chapters 10 and 11 will set forth some ways of measuring managerial growth and will finally restate our basic concepts.

One final point: In true OD fashion we do not believe that you will learn or understand the basic concepts and ideas which we are attempting to introduce in this book without relating these ideas in some way to your own organization. For this reason, some of the chapters will have a set of work sheets which we encourage you to complete as you go along. It is hoped that in this way your learning will be increased and you will more easily discover the applicability of our ideas.

2/Changes Affecting MD

It is my premise that the bureaucratic form of organization is out of joint with contemporary realities; that new shapes, patterns, and models are emerging which promise drastic changes in the conduct of the corporation and of managerial practices in general. In the next 25 to 50 years, we should witness, and participate in, the end of bureaucracy as we know it and the rise of new social systems better suited to twentieth century demands of industrialization.[1]

In this statement Warren Bennis emphasizes changes in managerial practices. If we accept his basic argument on the assumption that society and organizations are changing, we must then contend that human developmental processes in organizations are also changing. More specifically, we believe that the traditional processes of management development are rapidly getting "out of step" with organizational realities, thus calling for a new look at how managers develop and grow within organizations.

Human growth and development in large numbers of existing organizations, when examined closely, appear to be mysterious processes carried out on the basis of "good faith" under the guise of "well-designed" training and development programs. Such developmental activities in organizations encompass a variety of activities, programs, practices, policies, methods, and approaches. In such organizations, precisely how managers develop is unknown, except that it is believed that exposure to previously successful managers in some way transmits managerial competency to the "up-and-coming" manager. Determining how managers develop within many organizations is, at best, educated guesswork.

If this is true, then what is the correct way to develop managers?

In order to answer this question we must study the nature of the organization in which the MD process takes place. We must understand how organizational structures and processes work in terms of methods, practices, activities, communication processes, and basic structural relationships. However, before we can understand why organizations are designed the way they are, we need to step back and examine the nature of the tasks—and the kinds of people required to perform them—whose completion enables the organization to successfully achieve its goals and objectives. Furthermore, the character of the tasks is inseparably tied to the technology of the industry of which an organization is a part, just as the characteristics of the people who perform those tasks is largely determined by the society in which they live. In other words, we must understand the nature of the technology in which the organization is involved and the general societal factors which impinge upon it.

It seems clear, therefore, that before we can answer the question of how to train managers in a specific organization, we need to examine the character of the technical and societal environment in which the organizations function.

Our starting point in understanding management development processes is illustrated in Fig. 2.1. We will examine step-by-step the factors that we believe shape the character of an organization and its processes, and, therefore, the means by which managers can best be developed.

Figure 2.1

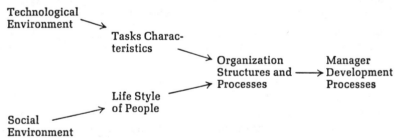

ENVIRONMENT

The environment in which an enterprise functions embraces both industrial technology and the society in which it operates. The technological environment in which the organization exists influences the nature of the tasks the organization performs and the problems it encounters. The latter include diffusion, changes and complexity of knowledge, and the handling of information important to the organization's survival. These factors in turn determine the work which must be done and the ways employees accomplish their work. On the other hand, the social environment in which the organization exists influences the values, needs, and perceptions of the organization's members. It includes cultural norms and values, how they are diffused, how they change, and their complexity—all of which are affected by societal influences and individual life styles.

Technology interacts with society, and vice versa. As technical changes affect the structure of our society, society becomes more aware of its technical environment (as with ecology, for example). The better educated we are, the more technology we develop, accelerating the rate of technological and societal change.

Examination of the technological aspects of our industrial environment shows that some industries are highly stable while others are rapidly changing. For example, the brewing industry has changed very little over the last several centuries, while the electronics industry (which didn't even exist a few decades ago) reveals phenomenal change during the last 30 to 40 years.

Organizations are an integral part of society and changes taking place in society have a direct causal relationship to organizations. The nature of our society a hundred years ago had a significant influence on the character of an organization then. Usually the better educated, smarter, and more rational people tended to be only at the top of an organization, while the more subservient, poorly educated people tended to be at the bottom of it. People at the bottom, it was assumed, did not want to be leaders, and were perfectly willing to be told what to do. They were expected to be obedient and to follow the dictates of those at the top. Such assumptions prevailed because the top people were better educated, because limited communication restricted the awareness of the masses, while nobility inherited leadership roles, and because the poor were willing to accept the subservient role in order to exist. As technology and education improved the social condition and awareness of the masses of people, the old concept of leadership by social class also started to change, and our society began to take on new values, to develop new attitudes about the roles of all its members. And as society and people changed, organizations began to change. Today the nature of our society and its members has a potent influence over how organizations function.

TASKS AND PEOPLE

Rapid and expansive changes in technology during the past 40 to 50 years, as well as the development of new societal characteristics, have led to changes in the tasks performed within organizations as well as in the nature of people working in organizations. Within a more traditional environment, where technology was stable and the upper classes inherited the right to lead, we found simple tasks being performed by obedient people. Such tasks required routine, standardized, and simple activities by those performing them. People were willing to accept authority and were usually highly loyal to their organizations. This loyalty and obedience grew out of their insecurity, in part the result of their immobility due to low educational levels and lack of awareness of opportunities outside their immediate surroundings. Furthermore, most working people in those times had grown up in a society which placed high value on work for its own sake.

The traditional life styles of people six to seven decades ago characterized the individual's patterns of needs, values, and perceptions which have been labeled Formalistic.[2] Formalistic people looked to higher authorities for direction, believed in following the rules and regulations of the organization, felt that it was unacceptable under almost any circumstance to deviate from the directives issued from above. Such people tended to be future-oriented in terms of their goals and plans.

Since the end of World War II notable changes have taken place in the tasks which are performed in a large number of organizations. Tasks have become increasingly more complex, which calls for a higher degree of collaboration among people who have highly specialized knowledge and skills. Employees in very many organizations may often find themselves in situations in which they must initiate and act on issues on the spot, without reference to higher authority. They may have to initiate immediate changes in methods and tasks in order to avoid major problems. One of the results of this change in work patterns has been the evolution of the Sociocentric[3] life style, in which people at work are more concerned with cooperative/collaborative relationships and with one another.

More recently there has emerged a third life style, referred to as Personalistic.[4] Many people in our society have become concerned with the here-and-now orientation toward life, and are actively attempting to apply what they know and have learned to their personal lives. They are more self-actualizing and want to see their skills fully utilized. They actively confront the methods and attitudes of the "establishment" (organizations) in an effort to make life more meaningful. Such people tend to be both individualistic and collaborative, oftentimes seeking closer associations within small groups while striving to develop their full potential. People with this newer life style are prone to reject authority, precedent, and the rules and policies of organizations and instead seek to find the right actions and processes for themselves. They are inclined to reject autocratic ways of directing people and to accept more collaborative relationships as well as to insist on more freedom to do the things that they believe are right for themselves.

ORGANIZATION STRUCTURE

We are all familiar with the nature of the bureaucratic structure, in which relationships between people and their work are prescribed and specified, and in which tasks and people are subdivided on the basis of functional specialization. In such organizations you will find a well-defined hierarchy of authority in which rules and procedures govern nearly all work situations and employees.

Where organizational tasks are simple and people more formalistic, a bureaucratic form of organization usually works effectively. In such organizations the power is seated at the top and those in authority pass their directions downward. There is little need for collaboration or the sharing of functions and ideas. Where only a few rule, loyalty is demanded, for it is necessary to accomplish the organization's goal. Competition is considered healthy even if it results in conflict. If conflict occurs it is controlled and regulated through various policies, procedures, and practices.

As tasks have become more complex and people more socio-centric and personalistic, a new kind of "organic" organizational structure has emerged. Such structures are fluid, involving a continuous redefinition and redesign of tasks resulting from interaction with various groups and people. Such organizations foster a unique network structure of activities, communications, authority paths, and decision-making systems. Interaction in such organizations consists of information and advice rather than instructions and directives. Authority is vested more in expertise than in designated roles. Relationships are more collaborative and involve shared decision-making, openness of communication, mutual goal-setting, and shared authority. Loyalty toward the organization is not so rigidly demanded, and a higher order of commitment evolves between people. Shared developmental discussions are formed, rather than unilateral evaluation. (Teams of employees develop and oftentimes become concerned with particular aspects of other functions. Such teams may be temporary in nature.) There is much less respect for the *position* normally held by higher authorities, and, instead, an increasing respect for the *individual* holding that position.

Given a rapidly changing environment, a movement from simple to more complex tasks, and a shift from formalistic to sociocentric and personalistic life styles, organizations have been forced to move from a bureaucratic structure to more organic structures. There is increasing evidence that organizations so structured that members can deal with their tasks in a way that helps the individual grow and develop (allowing self-actualization) provide a powerful source of social and psychological satisfaction. As societal and technological factors alter tasks and life styles, so must the organization structures be altered for people to derive fulfillment of their needs as they accomplish their organization's tasks.

Under the basic bureaucratic form of organization our MD processes have probably been fairly well suited to developing formalistic managers, people who have defined for them what is required in order to ascend to a position of leadership within the organization. However, as more organic structures continue to emerge, it is quite apparent that new manager development processes must be used. Such processes, we believe, have more to do with how the organization is designed and developed than with how a specific management training program is designed.

Bureaucratic Organization: An Example*

The Dashman Company is a large concern making many types of equipment for the armed forces of the United States. It has over 20 plants, located in the central part of the country, whose purchasing procedures have never been completely coordinated. In fact, the head office of the company has encouraged each of the plant managers to operate with their staffs as separate independent units in most matters. Late in 1960, when it began to appear that the company would face increasing difficulty in securing certain essential raw materials, Mr. Manson, the company's president, appointed an experienced purchasing executive, Mr. Post, as vice president in charge of purchasing, a position especially created for him. Mr. Manson gave Mr. Post wide latitude in organizing his job, and he assigned Mr. Larson as Mr. Post's assistant. Mr. Larson had served the company in a variety of capacities for many years, and knew most of the plant executives personally. Mr. Post's appointment was announced through the formal channels usual in the company, including a notice in the house organ published by the company.

One of Mr. Post's first decisions was to begin immediately to centralize the company's purchasing procedure. As a first step he decided that he would require each of the executives who handled purchasing in the individual plants to clear with the head office all purchase contracts which they made in excess of $10,000. He felt that if the head office was to do any coordinating in a way that would be helpful to each plant and to the company as a whole, he must be notified that the contracts were being prepared at least a week before they were to be signed. He talked his proposal over with Mr. Manson, who presented it to his board of directors. They appoved the plan.

* Reprinted with permission of Richard D. Irwin, Inc., from *Organizational Change and Development*, G. Dalton, P. Lawrence, and L. Greiner (eds.).

Although the company made purchases throughout the year, the beginning of its peak buying season was only three weeks away at the time this new plan was adopted. Mr. Post prepared a letter to be sent to the 20 purchasing executives of the company. The letter follows:

Dear_____,

The board of directors of our company has recently authorized a change in our purchasing procedures. Hereafter, each of the purchasing executives in the several plants of the company will notify the vice president in charge of purchasing of all contracts in excess of $10,000 which they are negotiating at least a week in advance of the date on which they are to be signed.

I am sure that you will understand and that this step is necessary to coordinate the purchasing requirements of the company in these times when we are facing increasing difficulty in securing essential supplies. This procedure should give us in the central office the information we need to see that each plant secures the optimum supply of materials. In this way the interests of each plant and of the company as a whole will best be served.

Yours very truly,

Mr. Post showed the letter to Mr. Larson and invited his comments. Mr. Larson thought the letter an excellent one, but suggested that, since Mr. Post had not met more than a few of the purchasing executives, he might like to visit all of them and take the matter up with each one of them personally. Mr. Post dismissed the idea at once because, as he said, he had so many things to do at the head office that he could not get away for a trip. Consequently he had the letters sent out over his signature.

During the two following weeks replies came in from all except a few plants. Although a few executives wrote at greater length, the following reply was typical:

Dear Mr. Post,

Your recent communication in regard to notifying the head office a week in advance of our intention to sign contracts has been received. This suggestion seems a most practical one. We want to assure you that you can count on our cooperation.

Yours very truly,

During the next six weeks the head office received no notices from any plant that contracts were being negotiated. Executives in other departments who made frequent trips to the plants reported that the plants were busy, and the usual routines for that time of year were being followed.[5]

Organic Organization: An Example

"It was shocking," says a TRW Systems engineer who served on a six-man task force set up to find ways to run his division with 15 percent fewer employees because of the aerospace recession. "We all knew that the reorganization we were recommending could mean any one of our jobs was at stake."

Top management accepted his group's proposal, rather than announce an across-the-board cut from on high, and layoffs followed. "No one was happy," he says grimly, "but, by and large, we all agreed it was a fair and straightforward job."

Novel as layoff-by-task force may be, the notion of letting managers and employees thrash out problems together is nothing new for the high technology aerospace operating group of TRW, Inc. During the past decade, TRW Systems, based in Redondo Beach, California, has evolved a unique management style. It has linked two intriguing and often controversial concepts: management by Matrix where work is organized around temporary teams, and organization development (OD), which uses behavioral science techniques, such as sensitivity training and confrontation sessions, to make those teams operate more efficently.

These management devices worked well when profits were growing at 15 percent a year. Now with the aerospace industry under siege, the systems group is out to prove that those same tools are just as valuable during austerity.[6]

SUMMARY

The objective of this chapter has been to establish the point that organizations are changing because our technical and social environments are changing. How manager development pro-

Fig. 2.2 Comparison of traditional and emerging factors affecting human development processes in organizations

Traditional Factors		Emerging Factors	
Technological Environment	**Sociological Environment**	**Technological Environment**	**Sociological Environment**
Stable	Low awareness of world events	Rapid change	High world awareness
Simple		Complex	
Limited base of knowledge	Work-oriented (Protestant Ethic)	Rapid expansion of knowledge base	Revolutionary
	Subservient		Complex social problem
			Affluent
↓	↓	↓	↓
Tasks	**People**	**Tasks**	**People**
Routine	Accepted authority	Complex	Here and now orientation
Standardized	Loyal	Highly technical	
Simple	Obedient	Specialized knowledge	Well-educated
Machine-like	Insecure		Self-actualizing
Clear objectives	Moderate education	Integrative	Collaborative
		Ambiguous goals	Rejects authority
			Confronting
↓	↓	↓	↓
Bureaucratic Organization Structure		**Organic Organization Structure**	
Power at top of organization		Continual redefinition of functions and roles	
Closed communication		Shared leadership	
Functional specialization		Collaborative relationships	
Clearly defined relationships		Open communication	
Competitive		Less restrictive policies and practices	
Well-developed system of rules and practices		Temporary organizational structure	
↓		↓	
Management Development		**Organization Development**	

cesses are designed is largely dependent on the character of the people and tasks to be performed within the organization. Organizational development concepts are more viable as ways to understand how managers grow and develop; these are some of our more traditional management development approaches.

Figure 2.2 presents a summary of how technical and social environment affects the process of developing managers in organizations.

The character of our society, the technological environment, the nature of tasks and people are shifting in a direction which more and more requires an organic structure. This in turn will have a significant effect on the human developmental processes. In Chapter 3 we will examine more closely how the development process might be tailored to enhance manager growth and development.

REFERENCES

1. Bennis, Warren, *Changing Organizations,* McGraw-Hill, 1966.
2. Bier, Thomas, Ph.d. Dissertation, Case Western Reserve University, 1967.
3. *Ibid.*
4. *Ibid.*
5. G. Dalton, P. Lawrence, L. Greiner, *Organizational Change and Development,* Homewood, Ill., Irwin, 1970.
6. "Team Work Through Conflict," *Business Week,* March 20, 1971, p. 44.

3/Opposing Assumptions Underlying MD

Management development within organizations is not an abstract process that can be plugged into any organization regardless of its tasks, its people, its methods, and its structure. If the nature and processes of a development program are alien to the nature and processes in the organization, it becomes at best an irrelevant program and, at a more serious level, a source of aggravation and frustration to the organizational system, not to mention the people in the organization. Development must be tailored to where the organization is as well as where it wants to be.

We shall pose four questions in this chapter, each of which is designed to help you explore the assumptions you have about your organization. The four questions are:

1. Where is the relevant knowledge in the organization?

2. How does the organization grow?

3. Is the organization a collection of individuals or a collaborative system?

4. What is the most appropriate learning process for the development and utilization of the organization's social and human resources?

The answers to these four questions may be drawn from one of two kinds of assumptions concerning the organization. One set of assumptions suggests a traditional MD program, the other suggests an OD approach. The final section of the chapter is a discussion of some cautions about—and opportunities revealed by—the answers to these questions.

WHERE IS THE RELEVANT KNOWLEDGE IN THE ORGANIZATION?

The first assumption concerns the location of the knowledge and skills in the organization which are relevant to the specific tasks and issues on which it is working. One assumption (that

---

This chapter was written by Dr. Frank Friedlander, of Case Western Reserve University.

of MD) is that the relevant operating and managerial knowledge is vested entirely in a few select members of a managerial elite somewhere at the top of the pyramid or at the top of sub-pyramids in the organizational hierarchy. Similarly, the knowledge for making changes in the organization and management is vested in these same positions. This set of assumptions suggests that development programs (MD) prepare people lower down in the organization to eventually enter responsible positions. Development becomes essentially a preparation for entry. The assumption that we can properly prepare people to enter elite positions is parallel to the assumption that we can properly select people for a managerial elite. Thus, where we find traditional MD programs, we frequently find a traditional emphasis on the use of psychological tests, assessment centers, and other management identification programs. The focus of these programs is not geared to particular organizational issues. Instead it is geared toward selecting an ideal man who can manage the organization. If we know what that typical ideal manager looks like in our organization, then we should be able to select future managers on this same basis, and then train them on this basis as well.

The alternative (OD) assumption about an organization is that the knowledge for its operation, management, and change is widely dispersed among its people and groups. Where this specialized knowledge lies depends on the specific tasks and issues at hand, and we may assume that it does not necessarily reside entirely at the top of the organization. We may also assume that the location of skill is constantly changing, since the tasks and issues are changing, and that the knowledge cannot be ascribed to a specific position or role, but rather to individuals and groups regardless of their formal place in the organization chart. Development and change, according to this assumption, is the responsibility of all employees in the organization; initiation and control is located in the people who have knowledge of the development issues. Thus, every employee is a potential manager, depending on the task or issue to be solved. This contrasts with our usual stereotype of management as an elite group occupying certain established positions at or near the top of the pyramid.

On the basis of this assumption, development programs must deal with here-and-now organization issues rather than prepare people to enter a managerial elite. They should provide people with problem-solving skills which can be used currently, and they should emphasize the collaborative skills needed for working in an organization in which knowledge and skills are widely dispersed rather than centrally located.

HOW DOES THE ORGANIZATION GROW?

A related set of assumptions concerns the basis for organizational growth. One assumption common to MD is that the organization grows by following and refining its current methods, procedures, and people. The basis for this assumption is that the organization has arrived at its current condition of success by using these already successful methods. While these may need small refinements, they don't need radical change. Therefore, development programs (MD) are most effective if they are focused on reinforcing established methods. Similarly, development programs need to refine people's thinking and help them brush up, thereby forming pools of ready talent that can fit into the current processes and structures of the organization.

The alternative (OD) assumption about organizations is that they grow by continually adapting and changing their methods and structures to meet new technologies and behavioral styles. Precedent will always lag behind current needs and demands. Development programs (OD) must provide learning about change —what to change, how to change—and practice in making changes.

IS THE ORGANIZATION A COLLECTION OF INDIVIDUALS OR A COLLABORATIVE SYSTEM?

On this subject, one assumption is that the organization is composed of separate individuals, each of them applying their effort, ideas, and skills regardless of the relationships they have with others in the organization and regardless of their perception of the organizational climate. This assumption suggests that the prime focus of development programs (MD) should be on individuals, and that their conceptual and social skill training will enhance their efforts, skills, and ideas. Thus, *individuals* need to develop and change, but the system in which they work does not. Individuals are developed as though there were no current organization systems of which they are a part. They can temporarily leave that system (physically and psychologically) to receive training, and then be returned to the system as more effective.

The alternative assumption is that the organization is composed of closely linked sets of people whose total knowledge and effort is more than the sum of its individuals. These close linkages and relationships require development just as much as do the individuals in them. Thus the basic issue for a development program is whether it focuses on *individual* development and change without regard to the employee's relationships back on the job (as MD does) or whether it must incorporate *system* changes so that both the system and the individual may develop and change concurrently. Organization development is concerned with the simultaneous development of both the individual and the intricate set of relationships which exist for him or her back on the job. The premise of OD is that change and development cannot occur within the individual without change in the organizational system. These system changes support and foster the development in the individual. Similarly, the individual feels greater influence in applying his or her development and learning to the organization and its issues.

WHAT IS THE MOST APPROPRIATE LEARNING PROCESS FOR THE ORGANIZATION?

Of course, the purpose of any organization's development program is to develop and utilize its social and human resources in the most effective manner. If the previously stated management development assumptions are valid (that we are developing and training employees for eventual entry into a management elite, that the organization grows by refining its methods and people, and that the individual needs development but the organizational system does not), then this suggests a fourth assumption concerning the learning and development process. This is that the most effective development can occur through the following sequence: (a) A curriculum is developed by those representing the philosophies and methods of the management elite; it is based on the historical precedents of the organization; it is "taught" to promising and potential managers. (b) The MD program is responsible for developing and teaching this curriculum; the participants in the program are responsible for absorbing and remembering it as best they can. (c) The relationship between teacher and learner is a traditional one in which the teacher is assumed to know what the problems are and what the answers are. (d) The teacher is active and knowledgeable, the student is passive and naive.

Of course, this approach does not preclude heated group discussions among teacher and student, but the intended curriculum is still the end point of the development sequence. The learning model can be pictured as follows:

Knowledge of
precedent and $\longrightarrow$ Teaching $\longrightarrow$ Learning $\longrightarrow$ Storage $\longrightarrow$ Eventual
management   usage
elite

Since the participants have had little chance to develop and participate in the curriculum, and little opportunity to apply their learnings to here-and-now organizational issues, evaluation of both the MD program and participants' learning must necessarily be based on how well the participants have stored their knowledge or how their ideas have been molded to fit in with the company's ideas. The follow-ups of MD programs usually consist of questionnaires, tests, and interviews, rather than studies of the degree to which the participants have applied their knowledge to immediate organizational issues or changed the organization in some way. Such tests, questionnaires, etc., are entirely appropriate, since clear criteria of what the participants should know were established prior to the program and were, therefore, built into the curriculum.

An entirely different learning model follows from the three OD assumptions we have already mentioned (that development must be concerned with actual here-and-now organizational issues and the collaborative skills needed for widely dispersed specialized knowledge, that development must provide learning about change through actual change in the organization, and that the focus of change must be on the organizational system rather than solely on the individual).

First, the OD learning model begins with helping individuals explore and increase their awareness of themselves (in the organization); who each is as a person and in relation to other people who are important to him or her in the work situation; the sources of their dissatisfaction and frustration (with themselves and with their performance); and what they would like to further explore and change in their own behaviors and in their relationships with others who are important to them on the job. When this awareness is achieved, each individual begins to plan action steps to explore with others these dissatisfactions and frustrations, determining who to discuss these issues with and what are the natural work situations (meetings, performance-evaluation sessions, team-building sessions, etc.) in which to act on these frustrations. The crucial step in the OD learning model is the "action step" actually taken by the participant. And finally, the participants initiate evaluation–research–learning through feedback from others to appraise their own actions and the impact of those actions on themselves and others. This awareness–action–research model can be pictured as follows:

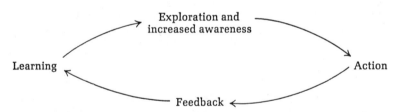

Note that the model is circular (rather than linear, as in the traditional model previously described). Learning creates increased awareness for further and perhaps different action, which leads to increased learning, and so on.

In addition, the OD learning model maximizes the individuals' sense of relevance, involvement, and responsibility. Since the issues for OD come from the individuals' own exploration and awareness, those issues are likely to be highly relevant to them. They become involved in all phases of the learning model: awareness–action–feedback. For example, the participants plan and seek out evaluation—which is a rare occurrence in the traditional learning model. In addition, they take prime responsibility for the action program—because the cause of their actions are their own (frustrations) and the learnings come from their own experience. They take the initiative to obtain feedback because they actively want to learn, so that they can become more aware and take more effective action on their own frustrations. Thus the participants are responsible for their own OD/MD program. The management development (MD) coordinator merely facilitates this learning process. Finally the OD learning model results in mutual learning rather than one-way teaching. Those coordinating OD programs are invariably influenced by the increased awareness of individuals about organizational issues and by the frustrations individuals are experiencing in their organizational settings. Similarly, employees not directly involved in the OD program are influenced and learn when program participants act on their increased awareness. And it is in this mutual-influence process in the actual work situation that OD tends to change and develop the system as well as the individual.

ASSUMPTIONS SOMETIMES GET CONFUSED

The two opposing sets of assumptions and the two types of development programs that match these assumptions are summarized in Table 3.1. The reader is advised to explore the methods and values of his or her own organization carefully before dismissing either set of assumptions as invalid. A number of development programs proceed on the basis of one set of assumptions only to find later that this decision was based on a vague unplanned hope rather than a reality shared by others.

There are a number of research studies concerning training programs which do not take into account the participants' organizational context and relationships and which treat them in isolation from this context. These studies generally indicate that such training programs fail. Flaishman (1953), for example, found that participants in a human-relations training program gained a more positive attitude toward a participative leadership style. But this favorable attitude declined to its pretraining level when the participants returned to their organizations, unless their superiors also shared this same attitude. Friedlander (1971) found that a social-skills training program for hard-core unemployed had no impact on their performance or retention after job placement; the only thing that did affect their performance and retention was the degree to which the work climate was a supportive one. In both cases, attitude changes resulting from training were temporary and nontransferable from the training situation to the organizational situation. Sometimes, however, individuals do maintain their changed behavior, but the organization cannot tolerate this. Sykes (1962), for example, found that a development program for supervisors which was not congruent with the goals and relationships of its top management caused a number of the supervisors to decide to leave the organization soon after the program was completed.

In the case of OD programs, there must be an agreement between the designers of the development program and those in relevant influential management positions that the development process is part and parcel of the organization process—that the MD/OD program is to be directly applied to immediate organizational issues, that the exploration of these issues will be a crucial part of the program, and that changes in organizational methods, relationships, and personal styles may well follow. The best way to keep the program goals and management goals congruent is to include relevant managers in the OD process.

Once the development programs which match organizational goals are in progress, they become meaningful and highly relevant processes for growth—of both the individual and the organization. Those in the program know that the organization is with them in their developmental efforts and ready to apply their learnings, and the organization senses a relevance and high regard for the development program.

We have attempted to create a mild dissonance in your mind so you will be willing to explore an alternate approach to MD. We are advocates of designing MD processes appropriate to the organizational processes. The question for the reader should be, "What is my organization like?" If you understand this, you can design MD activities and programs to fit the organization, or the organization can be arranged in a direction appropriate to the social and technical environment in which it finds itself.

The remainder of this book will attempt to examine organizational processes and to help you decide what developmental processes best fit your organization.

Table 3.1 Assumptions about organizations—and the resulting conclusions about developmental efforts in those organizations

---

Organizational Assumptions Leading to Management Development (MD)

---

1. *Assumption:* The knowledge for managing and changing the organization is vested in specified positions—usually at or near the top of the organization.

Therefore, development is most effective if it trains people for eventually entering these positions, particularly those in which they will need to make major decisions, set pervasive policies and goals for others in the organization, evaluate and control methods to attain these goals, and develop keen human-relations skills to accomplish all this. Development should be initiated by, controlled by, and is the responsibility of top management for the rest of the organization.

2. *Assumption:* The organization grows and develops by following its successful precedent and by refining its methods and structures.

Therefore, development is most effective if people learn about precedent, brush up on the latest skills so as to deal with precedent more effectively, and form pools of usable talent.

3. *Assumption:* The organization is composed of a collection of separate individuals, each of whom apply their ideas, efforts, and skills regardless of the relationships they have with others or the climate in which they work. Individuals work and develop regardless of the system of which they are a part.

Therefore, development is most effective if it focuses on the individual as an isolated unit. His or her relationships with people in the work situation and perception of what it's like to work in that particular organizational unit are irrelevant.

4. *Assumptions:* Appropriate knowledge and attitudes can result in effective behavior. The knowledge about "how the organization should be run" is already established. These things should be taught to organizational members. The members should be evaluated (on how well they learned "how the organization should be run"), but the knowledge (about "how the organization should be run") should not be evaluated. The learning process should reflect management functions: instruct, direct, and control. The relationship between instructor and participant should be like that between superior and subordinate.

Therefore, development is most effective if the knowledge based on organizational precedent and reflecting the ideas of the management elite is taught by instruction, learned by organizational members, and stored by them for eventual usage.

Organizational Assumptions Leading to Organization Development (OD)

1. *Assumption:* The knowledge for managing and changing the organization exists throughout the organization, and depends on the issue or task it faces.

Therefore, development is most effective if it helps people act on current organizational issues, particularly those in which increased problem-solving and collaborative team skills are needed in order to link up dispersed and specialized knowledge throughout the organization. Development and change should be initiated by, controlled by, and is the responsibility of any member of the organization, if he or she has knowledge which is relevant to an issue or problem facing the organization.

2. *Assumption:* The organization grows and develops by continually changing and adapting its methods and structures to new technologies and to new behavioral styles.

Therefore, development is most effective if people learn about change through actual change efforts in their current organizational situations.

3. *Assumption:* The organization is composed of closely linked sets of people whose total knowledge and efforts are more than the sum of its individuals. How they see their relationships and the climate they work in severely affects their work. Individuals cannot work and develop independently of the system of which they are a part.

Therefore, development is most effective if it focuses on development and change in the individual's organizational system. His or her awareness of the system and how to change relationships with others and the climate of the work unit are an integral part of his or her own development.

4. *Assumptions:* Behavior (both effective and ineffective) can result in learning which results in appropriate knowledge and attitudes. The knowledge about "how the organization should be run" is uncertain and varies among individuals. So that the resources of these individuals may be drawn on for effective change, they need to focus their frustrations, become involved in the management and change processes, and learn by initiating changes and obtaining feedback from others on the impact of their efforts. The learning process should reflect management functions: advise, consult, facilitate. Relationships in the development process should be characterized as those of collaboration and mutual learning.

Therefore, development is most effective if it emerges from the individual's own awareness, efforts to change his or her work relationships and climate, and feedback from those involved with him or her in this effort.

4/Framework for Evaluating MD Processes

When human development processes in organizations match organizational goals, then the developmental experiences become more meaningful and relevant to the individuals' personal growth and, therefore, their motivation and desire for change and self-improvement are enhanced. Up to this point we have examined some historical aspects of the developmental process in organizations and studied and discussed the assumptions which are often made about organizational structure, tasks, and processes. Now we would like to set forth a way to study an organization which will provide us with a definitive picture of how the organizational processes relate to individual development. Given that we understand organizational processes, we should then be able to design appropriate learning processes to match the organization's goals, structures, and tasks.

In this chapter we will discuss an organizational framework for viewing change. We will also compare the MD model with an OD approach to individual change.

A FRAMEWORK FOR VIEWING ORGANIZATION AND INDIVIDUAL CHANGE

The basic framework for viewing change that we intend to use is an OD change strategy. Organization development discussed in this context is used as a strategy for exploring life styles, the tasks that individuals must perform, and the basic structures complementary to both the life styles and tasks. We are concerned with how to match life styles, tasks, and organizational structures in order to optimize individual development (manager development).

An OD approach to development of managers is a system-oriented approach involving individually oriented developmental processes (see Fig. 4.1). To put it another way, it is a self-instigated approach to development when individuals explore and do things to change themselves in a direction meaningful to both themselves and the organization.

Organization development, when used in a broader organization sense, often involves the following steps:

1. Exploration of the problems facing the organization/group/ team.

Fig. 4.1 OD as a process for organizational change compared with processes for individual change

Organizational Change	Individual Change
1. Identify problem	1. Identify desired change
2. Diagnose problem	2. Diagnose blocks to change
3. Plan action	3. Plan action steps
4. Inform others outside problem areas	4. Enlist assistance from others
5. Initiate change	5. Initiate change
6. Feedback	6. Feedback

2. Getting organization members together to examine the problems facing their organization.

3. Working together in planning action steps and leverage points for change within the organization.

4. Widening the circle of change and influence in order to bring about viable and realistic change.

5. Instigating the changes.

6. Collecting data and feedback relative to the success of the change.

7. Planning future action steps and changes on the basis of immediate past experiences.

This same model, we believe, can be applied to individual changes as well. Applying OD processes to individual development and change, the individual would:

1. Explore basic problems which he or she is facing and develop an increased awareness of the things he or she would like to change.

2. Work out (using organizational resources) approaches which might be used to solve the problem or reach desired goals.

3. Develop action steps for making change.

4. Enlist the assistance of others within the organization to help bring about change.

6. Get feedback and information from others in the organization on how the new change is working.

7. Plan the next action step, going through essentially the same processes.

Basically, the individual is going through the following five developmental steps (essentially the same model described in Chapter 3):

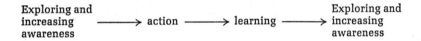

Exploring and increasing awareness ⟶ action ⟶ learning ⟶ Exploring and increasing awareness

The OD learning process is a more natural learning model. It is essentially the same model we see in infants and children as they are growing up. In our society, as children began to expand their awareness and increase their learning and explorations, adults start to make decisions for them relative to what they should and should not do. This continues throughout the schooling process and on into adulthood, which in effect subdues the more natural learning of which each person is capable. We are suggesting that using an OD model will produce a more self-directed learning which is beneficial both to the individual and the organization.

Keep in mind that the OD model for learning may not be appropriate for all organizations, and that the basic objective in this book is to help managers explore what is the best approach to learning and development for their particular organization—given the types of life styles which its members hold, the types of tasks which the organization performs and the type of structure used to control the individuals as well as the tasks which they are performing.

DIFFERENCES BETWEEN MD AND OD APPROACHES TO DEVELOPMENTAL PROCESSES

To enlarge our understanding of the differences between management development and organizational development as it applies to our discussion, we would like to make a comparison of a number of different aspects of both (Fig. 4.2).

Fig. 4.2 Comparison of MD and OD as they relate to human growth processes

Management Development	Organization Development
1. Packaged programs	1. Experience-based
2. Responsibility of staff personnel	2. Responsibility of individual
3. Inflexible	3. Flexible
4. Individual adapts to organization	4. Individual and organization change together
5. Safe, predictable	5. Risky, unpredictable
6. Individual is passive and inactive	6. Individual is involved and active in own learning
7. Highly cognitive (stockpiling information)	7. Cognition and behavior oriented

First of all, the developmental processes, as usually defined in an MD situation, are for the most part self-contained in the training programs. That is, they are usually found in MD programs, courses, and seminars. Contrasted with this, OD involves open and free experiences associated with daily living and work. With OD the individual may or may not attend courses, depending on how they fit his own needs and choices. He is free to make these choices on his own.

Second, the responsibility for MD program processes and systems is usually invested in the hands of an MD staff member. On the other hand, an OD approach gives the responsibility to the individual, or in some cases the group of people to which the individual is looking for advice and guidance.

Third, under an MD approach, systems and programs remain constant over an extented period of time. That is, once programs are established they stay established over extended periods of time. But OD is flexible and pliable; there is a high degree of change, which occurs frequently and often quite rapidly. Under MD the individual must adapt to the system; in OD, the individual changes while the system is also changing. In fact, the individual helps to bring about the change in the system.

Fourth, in MD it is assumed that the individual must accept and adapt to the requirements of the organization. In this case each person is expected to follow a prescribed set of guidelines to enhance his or her development. In OD, however, both the organization and the individual are adaptive. In fact, each influences the other to the advantage of both.

Fifth, MD processes are relatively safe. They assume that the individual will perform effectively within the context of the programs and procedures which are prescribed. On the other hand, OD processes tend to be more risky. The individual may, in fact, experiment with particular learning opportunities and find that they are not suitable for himself or herself. Or, one may develop a particular interest in a field which is not appropriate to the interests of the organization.

Sixth, under an MD approach the individual tends to assume the role of a passive participant; somewhat withdrawn from the organization. He or she tends to sit back and let things happen, to be uncreative and make relatively few contributions to the design of the MD system itself. Contrasted with this, OD processes require a high degree of involvement of the individual. Each participant is actually very much in it and a part of the process in terms of his or her own learning as well as learning for the organization.

Seventh, MD training is highly cognitive; the participant is oriented to storing data and information to be used at some future point in his or her career. Organization development processes, on the other hand, are action-oriented, resulting in immediate change and learning. Not only does OD involve cognition, but it is focused on behavior change.

Again we would caution that the OD model for learning may not be appropriate for all organizations. It is quite likely, however, that many organizations would find that their human developmental processes could be more productive if they were more OD oriented.

A PRACTICAL WAY TO LOOK AT AN ORGANIZATION

As stated earlier, we are attempting to provide you with a useful way to analyze your own organization so you can design relevant manager development processes. Analysis of your organization should be aimed at maximization of the learning and developmental processes for each individual. In order to achieve this result we have created a framework which we intend to use as a construct for the remainder of this book. Figure 4.3 introduces a starting framework for viewing types of organizations and how they change. Here we will be looking at three basic types of organizational structures: the *boss-centered* organization, or bureaucratic structure, the *group-centered* or collaborative approach, and the *individual-centered* or coordinative organizational structure. We believe that there are certain job-related and management development processes which these three types of organizations carry on. Furthermore, we feel that certain behavioral responses of the organizations are quite predictable. For example, in a boss-centered organization you can expect to see people conforming to the rules; you can expect their behavior to be highly predictable; you can anticipate that they will be nonadaptive and somewhat noncreative. In contrast, people in an individual-centered organization are likely to be nonconforming (that is, they may show many different responses to similar situations); their behavior will be unpredictable, adaptive, and highly creative. In an approach to manager development, we start by asking ourselves, "Where is my organization, and where do we want it to go?" As you will see later, the model we are proposing is designed to assist you in answering these questions.

For now let's take a limited example. Suppose your organization is at point X on the line (see Fig. 4.3). After you have examined the basic technology and major tasks in your organization, you conclude that you would like to see your organization move from point A to point B. You can then move back up

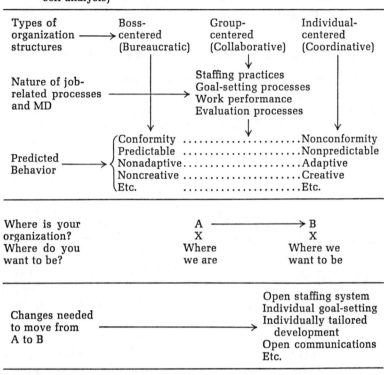

Fig. 4.3 Planned learning and developmental processes (organizational self-analysis)

Types of organization structures ⟶	Boss-centered (Bureaucratic)	Group-centered (Collaborative)	Individual-centered (Coordinative)

Nature of job-related processes and MD ⟶ Staffing practices / Goal-setting processes / Work performance / Evaluation processes

Predicted Behavior ⟶

Conformity ....Nonconformity
Predictable ....Nonpredictable
Nonadaptive.....................Adaptive
Noncreative ....Creative
Etc. ....Etc.

Where is your organization?
Where do you want to be?

A ⟶ B
X   X
Where   Where we
we are   want to be

Changes needed to move from A to B ⟶

Open staffing system
Individual goal-setting
Individually tailored development
Open communications
Etc.

through the model to examine the types of job-related processes and the practices which you would need to have in order to effectively develop people at point B.

We realize that there are numerous risks involved in the approach which we are suggesting. Perhaps some of these are worth a brief discussion.

1. It is quite possible that some parts of our model are incorrect and are simply not appropriate to your organization. For example, we may have placed too much stress on that of a contributing job-related process. In fact, it may have a very limited effect on the developmental outcomes, where another factor

may have much greater impact. In other words, we have not attempted to weigh the relative importance of the various job-related processes, and this could distort the results produced.

2. Through your own interpretation you may misunderstand what the model is. Secondly, you may misread what is actually going on in your own organization. However, this particular risk is with us all of the time; we can only hope to sharpen our skills in analyzing our organization.

3. The general model which we are setting forth may be satisfactory from an overall point of view and its application may meet most of the individual needs within the organization, but it may, in fact, miss the mark totally for a selected or specific individual.

4. Organizations are ever-changing and dynamic in their nature. What you see today—or what you saw yesterday—may be quite different tomorrow or sometime in the future. Therefore, whatever learning and developmental approaches you design at this time may be inappropriate for the future.

5. An improper assessment of the organization and resulting changes may stimulate unwanted and undesirable consequences.

Most of these risks are within the range of normal day-to-day risks which we all take in our daily activities and in the process of making decisions. Therefore, we urge you to not let them discourage you. We believe the approach we are suggesting will provide you with a more organized approach to designing human developmental processes in your organization.

The greatest advantage of the model which we are about to present is that it does offer a systematic and organized way of studying organizational processes in terms of how people develop and grow. It should produce a more accurate assessment and in turn help you to design a more viable learning and developmental approach, thereby producing an environment in which people can develop and learn that is appropriate to the organizational context in which they find themselves.

AN ANALYTICAL MODEL FOR EVALUATING AND DESIGNING MD PROCESSES

In Fig. 4.4 we summarize the total framework which we are proposing to follow for the remainder of this book. This model outlines the basic variables which we are going to examine. You will note that the various cells are not filled. We plan to take each of the contributing job-related processes and management development practices and examine them in terms of the mediating organizational variables for the various types of organizations. As we do this we will fill in the various cells one-by-one. (The Appendix shows this model expanded, with a separate form for each of the three organizational structures.)

Definitions. We would like to define the various terms which will be used in our discussions. We will start with the various types of organizational structure, which includes a bureaucratic structure, a collaborative structure, and a coordinative structure. Following Friedlander's (1970) description, the bureaucratic structure may be defined as one in which the relationships between people and their work are prescribed and specified. In such a structure, tasks and people are subdivided on a basis of functional specialization in which a well-defined hierarchy of authority exists and in which a system of rules and procedures governs and protects nearly all work situations and employees. The collaborative structure refers to a structure in which different people are working on the same subtask. In some cases, positions have joint responsibility for certain tasks. (For example, as in a tug-of-war team, or in riding a tandem bicycle.) The tasks performed by various groups in a collaborative structure are the joint responsibility of all the people in the group and require members to work together concurrently. A coordinating structure refers to a structure in which the tasks are allocated to different people. For example, the subtask may be sequenced in such a way that each person works autonomously. If necessary, outputs from these subtasks are subsequently integrated at some point down the line. Coordination structures involve group integration through dividing the group subtasks, which are ordered by definite precedent relationships. The subtasks may be allocated to the various positions. Group members

Fig. 4.4 Framework for outline of basic MD variables

Job-related processes contributing to MD	Types of Organizational Structure											
	Bureaucratic (Med. org. variables)			Collaborative (Med. org. variables)			Coordinative (Med. org. variables)		
	Auth.	Info.	Rel.	Auth.	Info.	Rel.	Auth.	Info.	Rel.
Staffing processes									
Goal-setting processes									
Work performance									
Evaluation processes									
MD practices									
Programs, systems, procedures, policies									
Behavior outputs									
Behavior to be expected from individual									

Auth. = Authority paths and decision processes
Info. = Information flow and information systems
Rel. = Individual and organizational relationships

cooperate not by concurrently sharing the same tasks, but by coordinating their tasks so that their flow is smooth and continuous.

Mediating organizational variables. In our model we choose to use mediating organizational variables because they appear to be the primary factors which mediate the way in which the organization functions. Therefore, they have a primary influence over how people develop. *Authority paths and decision processes* have to do with how people report to each other, who is responsible for what, how work assignments are determined and delegated within the organization, the policies and procedures related to informing and maintaining the organizational integrity, and, finally, how and at what level decisions are made in the organization. The second group of mediating organizational factors involve *information flow and information systems*. These relate to how information moves within the organizational context. For example, it may move from the top of the organization systematically through each level to the bottom. Or it may flow both downward and upward through the system. It may also flow in many directions, depending on the need that various individuals have for information. The information system may be described as the procedures and approaches which the organization designs for the purpose of disseminating information. One dimension of this is the degree to which an individual is allowed—or not allowed—to have certain kinds of information. In a closed-information system, for example, the information given to an individual is carefully screened and sorted, and only certain data are allowed to filter to the individual. In an open system, the individual has complete and free access to all information.

The final mediating organizational variable (individual and organizational relationships) is a somewhat more difficult one to define. It has to do with the individual within the organization and his or her relationships with other individuals, as well as the overall organizational relationships. In this factor we are looking at how people unite within the organization, how they handle conflict, how they cooperate, and how they handle the interdependency that they have on one another. Furthermore, we are interested in the level of trust and the amount of loyalty that an individual or organizational component has for the total organization and how individuals within the organization help one another.

Contributing job-related processes. We believe that there are four basic job-related processes. Each makes a major contribution to the developmental and learning processes in an organization. They are *staffing processes, goal-setting processes, work-performance processes,* and the *evaluation and feedback processes.* Staffing processes relate to how people obtain jobs and move from one position to another within the organizational context. On the one hand, the individual may typically be selected by his or her boss and be given no opportunity to participate in that decision. On the other hand, the individual may evaluate his or her own candidacy and decide where and when he or she wishes to apply for a promotion or a new position.

Goal-setting processes have to do mainly with who decides what an individual's work goals will be and how they are defined. For example, in a bureaucratic structure you might expect that the manager in charge would decide what constitutes a satisfactory job and communicate standards of performance to those people working for him or her. This contrasts with the coordinative system, in which the individual determines what his or her goals are in light of the goals of others with whom he or she is coordinating and in light of the objectives of the total organization.

Work-performance processes define what and how work is performed in terms of its scope—that is, the extensiveness or degree of specialization, as well as the extent to which the individual is free to determine how he or she will do the job.

The last factor, evaluation processes, relates to the ways in which individuals learn how effectively they are performing their work. On the one hand, a boss may be making a subjective judgmental decision about a person's performance, while on the other hand, the individual may be making judgments about his or her performance in terms of goals which he or she has personally set in conjunction with the boss.

Management development practices. In this particular part of our model we are concerned with looking at the actual programs, practices, procedures, systems, policies, and approaches used within an organization which seem to be compatible with the various types of organization structure. In a bureaucratic structure, as previously mentioned, we would expect that knowledge of precedents within the organization would be taught to individuals, who would be expected to store such knowledge for eventual use. In the coordinative structure, we would expect that individuals would explore and increase their own self-awareness, take action on the basis of it, and receive feedback for themselves out of which comes their learning and increased exploration and self-awareness.

Behavioral outputs. In the final part of our model we are attempting to define how a person can be expected to behave given the various job-related processes within one of the three types of organizational structures. The behavioral outputs are expressed in terms of conformity, predictability, adaptiveness, creativeness, dependency, information-sharing, openness, and helping others.

You will note that we have left out of the model any direct reference to the nature of the individuals within the organization. That is, we have not discussed life styles and their compatibility with organization structure. We are assuming for the purposes of our discussion that life styles are compatible within a given organization context. Thus it would not be difficult for a person with a formalistic life style to follow the job-related processes and MD programs established in a bureaucratic organization. We are not so naive as to believe that all people fit the organization perfectly. We recognize that people within organizations are to some degree incongruent with the organization structure and processes.

EXAMINING YOUR ORGANIZATION

Using the contributing job-related processes as our major headings, we will proceed to study each of them as they vary for different types of organizations and as mediating organizational variables influence them.

At the end of each of Chapters Five through Eight you will find a work sheet and scoring instrument which we encourage you to use to analyze, evaluate, and describe your own organization. You will receive more information on this activity at the end of each chapter.

As you no doubt have concluded by now, we show a strong preference for the more organic learning model (described in Chapter 3). Thus we have designed this book in a way which we hope will increase your awareness and encourage you to explore in such a way that you will be willing to take action within your own organization. Hopefully, when you have finished reading this book you will have developed a picture of your organization which should be helpful in guiding you in deciding where you would like to see your organization move and what kinds of changes you would like to see take place. In other words, the objective we are attempting to accomplish is to help you see where your management development processes and job-related processes may be inconsistent or incongruent with each other.

If you can see this, it is our hope that you will then be able to make adjustments in the various factors affecting learning and development, and that these adjustments will result in your increased effectiveness and individual growth and development within your organization.

5/Staffing Processes

In this chapter we examine the basic characteristics of staffing processes as they relate to management development. Here we are concerned with that portion of our model related to how individuals are most likely to be placed, transferred, and promoted in organizations which have bureaucratic, collaborative, or coordinative structures. For each structure we will study staffing processes first by looking at the authority paths and decision-making processes involved, then by seeing how staffing information flows within an organization and what systems are provided for that flow, and then by examining the individual and organizational relationships involved.

We remind you that this is only one part of a total model that we are going to examine, and that when the whole model is assembled it should give you some insight about the best approach to MD in your organization. At the end of this chapter we will give you the opportunity to judge your own organization relative to the descriptive variables discussed here.

BUREAUCRATIC STRUCTURE

Authority Paths and Decision Processes

You will recall that authority paths and decision processes have to do with how people report to each other, who is responsible for what, and how work (job) assignments are determined or delineated within the organizational context. These processes also involve policies, procedures, and practices related to forming and maintaining organizational integrity, as well as to how and at what levels decisions are made within the organization.

In bureaucratic structures managers are encouraged to develop personal awareness of the qualifications and competencies of their staffs. They are encouraged to be "developers" of people by having those people emulate the basic management patterns which the members of the managerial organization are currently following. The reason for this is that any manager who wants to move up will sooner or later be called on to help select his or her own understudy/replacement. In the bureaucratic structure this is principally the manager's own job; it is not shared with subordinates.

In general, individuals have virtually nothing to say about which opportunities they will be considered for. They cannot even choose *not* to be considered. In this type of organization people are not likely to be promoted from one functional area to another (i.e., Manufacturing to Sales); instead they usually find that their growth and opportunity paths rest primarily in the functional specialties in which they are currently involved.

In a bureaucratic staffing system, procedures and policies relative to individual growth and development tend to be generalized into broad policy statements. For example: "This organization promotes from within on a nondiscriminatory basis, following a standard requisitioning procedure and usually working directly with an employment manager to fill openings." This is abbreviated, of course, but the message is clear to managers: "Follow the rules," and "Keep it secret."

The personnel department in a bureaucratic organization usually is of no positive help to the disaffected employee, since it is more likely to serve as a "wailing wall" or "chaplain's office" than as a place where something constructive can be done about the employee's problems. The result is more complaint counseling than placement counseling, in which individuals who have been denied opportunities are soothed into returning to the job and accepting the fact that they were not promoted.

Information Flow and Information Systems

This subject relates to how information moves within an organization, whether that be from top to bottom, downward and upward simultaneously, or in several directions at once. Information systems may be described as the procedures and approaches designed by an organization for the purpose of disseminating business information internally. They also determine the extent to which the individuals within an organization are allowed—or not allowed—to receive certain data relevant to the organization, their departments, and their jobs. In a closed system, for example, employees are given very little information; in an open system they are given considerable opportunity to sift and sort the information necessary for the performance of their jobs.

The information system of a bureaucratic structure requires

that managers seek out data and information concerning job candidates whom they would like to consider for possible opportunities in their departments. Keep in mind, however, that most of the information each manager seeks relates to those people working directly for him or her. It is generally unacceptable for managers to go outside of their organizations for information about possible candidates for promotion. To do so is considered a weakness on the part of those managers, since it reflects on how well they have developed their staffs.

Generally, the individual members of an organization are not aware of opportunities within their own departments (assuming a large department), except as positions become visible following terminations, deaths, etc. They are also almost totally unaware of openings elsewhere in the company except as the grapevine or informal information system makes them aware.

There are usually no formal organizational systems or procedures for identifying the various competencies and skills of individuals. Bureaucratic structures tend to have incomplete personnel files and generally no data storage systems such as a computer or Kardex type system.

Individual and Organizational Relationships

In any type of organization, bureaucratic or otherwise, when the goals and values of the employees agree with those of the organization it is highly probable that employee behavior will be consistent with that expected by the organization. In a bureaucratic organization this means that the employees will learn the rules, regulations, policies, and practices established by the organization and adhere to them closely and in a highly predictable manner. They will learn well by rote, but may find it difficult to apply their knowledge unless the opportunity to do so occurs soon after the learning process. They will not be particularly adaptive and may find it difficult to adjust to changes either inside or outside of the organization—even though the need for and requirements of those changes are clearly understood.

Workers in this type of organization usually look to the organization's procedures and policies when they are in need of information, or to informed sources such as managers or department heads. They often distort available information to suit their own needs, and go to the "rumor mill" for information that is otherwise lacking. And to complete the picture they often fill in the gaps with their own hunches and guesses.

The employees in a bureaucratic structure often compete with each other for the jobs they would like. This leads to a certain amount of political maneuvering and apple-polishing—and back-biting as well. Such activity may be beneficial to an employee if it results in making him or her highly visible to the manager in a favorable light, for the bureaucratic manager's tendency is to promote the person who is most highly and favorably visible. And in a bureaucratic organization it is the manager who determines who will be promoted. Employees who disagree with the manager's policy of promotion (or transfer) may be ignored—or they may find that they have actually jeopardized their future employment.

The bureaucratic structure requires that the manager enforce rules and crack down on disagreements; presentation of different viewpoints is discouraged and often not even allowed. Individual workers are not encouraged to exercise their own discretion or to show initiative. As a result, they tend to hold back, and not assist the manager in solving any problem until specifically asked to do so. Bureaucratic managers are often surprised to discover what highly constructive and useful ideas employees have kept to themselves because "nobody asked me."

The tendency of workers to hold back is shown in other ways as well. Those who feel that they have been treated unfairly are likely to respond in one of two ways: to quit their job or, much more commonly, to withdraw from it—that is, to hold back and put no more of themselves into the job than is absolutely necessary to get by. This, of course, has serious effects on both the quantity and quality of production.

COLLABORATIVE STRUCTURE

Authority Paths and Decision Processes

In the collaborative structure the final decision on promotions rests with the manager, just as in the bureaucratic structure. However, the method of reaching that decision is much different in the collaborative structure. There, the peers of the person being considered for the promotion are often consulted for their opinions of the candidate's management potential, and information can be obtained from the personnel department as well.

While workers tend to show a low degree of trust and confidence in the objectivity and fairness of the staffing system, they show a fairly high degree of trust in the judgments made by one member of the organization about another. Partly because of this the person promoted is often the one who is best liked by the group. He or she may or may not be the most competent person, but is usually the one who has developed the greatest interpersonal skills and used them most effectively within the organization.

Those who are promoted in the collaborative organization are usually chosen on the basis (besides popularity) of the loyalty and service they have demonstrated in the past. They are usually advanced within their department or specialty, not moved from one to another. They are allowed to express their job preferences, but this probably has little effect on the promotion decision. Those being promoted are told that it is a collective decision and asked how they feel about the idea, but it is assumed that they will respond favorably. If they do, that settles it. If they do not, and have a legitimate reason for their negative response, or raise questions, the manager can usually resolve the problem with some form of sales talk and a little help from higher echelons.

Staffing policies in a collaborative organization involve an elaborate set of procedures (how-to's) which the manager must follow. The personnel department, which functions as a resource reservoir and not as a decision-making body, usually has a central data system which the manager can use. This system (computerized, Kardex, etc.) provides information on the background, experience, education, and performance of the candidate for promotion. Employees interested in jobs in other departments are usually not provided with information, but information does flow freely between various members of different departments.

Although the personnel department may play some role in job counseling, the individual turns to his or her own group for assistance, guidance, and feedback. Since the selection process is influenced by the group, the person seeking advancement must have their support, and gains it by following the advice of those group members who have the most influence.

Information Flow and Information Systems

In collaborative organizations individuals share ideas and suggestions where such sharing appears to be of benefit to the group or the organization. The result is a pool of information about the talents and skills of organization members that is useful in the making of decisions about advancement and promotion. The search for information through the organization's formal information system is continuous, but oftentimes more reliance is placed on informal channels. The latter fact allows a relatively high degree of distortion, because the individuals supplying the informal information are not themselves fully informed, and must fill in the gaps from their own general knowledge (which may be inaccurate or incomplete) or their imagination. Information flow in this system suffers from what is not available more than from what is.

Individual and Organizational Relationships

Individuals in a collaborative structure tend to behave in a predictable manner; however, their primary guides to behavior are not organizational policies, procedures, and practices, but rather the norms established by their own group, as well as by other groups in the organization. To understand individual behavior, therefore, it is necessary to understand the group norms. These norms dictate that, among other things, individuals must rely on the assistance of their peers and the group processes in order to acquire the knowledge and support they need to move ahead.

Although individuals do express their feelings and desires, they are expected to subordinate their will to that of the group; this is good group behavior. When there is conflict between one group and another, loyalty to one's own group is essential. Conversely, individuals may freely call on the group for assistance with their own problems. Those who tend not to follow the group norms are informally disciplined in various ways, up to and including removal from the group.

Members of a collaborative organization tend to be adaptive to changes made within their groups, but less so to changes made by other groups; and they are much less adaptive to changes outside the organization itself.

COORDINATIVE STRUCTURE

Authority Paths and Decision Processes

The manager in a coordinative organizational structure plays a far less significant role in staffing than in the other two structures we have discussed. To begin with, when an opening occurs in any group, the manager of that group requests the personnel department to post a notice of the opening throughout the organization so that any individual in the organization who is interested may apply for it. This includes people in other groups and specialties; for the coordinative organization's policy is that this encourages the development of more broadly experienced managers.

Every person in the organization has the right to recommend himself or herself for promotion to any opening he or she wants. Thus the next step in the promotion process occurs when someone decides to go for the new opening. The individual can apply directly to the manager in whose group the opening has occurred, or application can be made through the personnel department. If the individual would like more information before making application, he or she may obtain it from those same sources. This system is well defined, though it has many variations. The candidate is not required to get permission from his or her boss before making application.

The controlling policies and procedures of a coordinative organizational structure are broad, simple, and loosely defined, allowing for considerable latitude, judgment, and interpretation on the parts of both the candidate for the job and the manager with the job opening. The latitude is not so broad, however, that the candidate can also make the selection decision. That is still done by the manager in conjunction with others who are in a position to be objective about the applicant's capabilities. In most cases, this means that the job goes to the person best qualified to fill it; loyalty and length of service are not primary considerations. This policy also has the effect of reducing conflict and increasing cooperation, for it is known that the basis of the selection was competency, not politics.

In a coordinative system, then, the individuals' personal goals become primary. All individuals can evaluate their own competencies, interests, and motivations as honestly and objectively as possible and place themselves into or out of consideration for advancement. The organization's coaching and counseling is performed not only by the personnel department, but also the individual's own managers, peers, contacts outside the organization, and the manager to whom application is being made. Each individual collects information about his or her own competency and abilities through all available sources.

Information Flow and Information Systems

In the coordinative structure both formal and informal information sources make accurate information freely available to all members of the organization who seek it. Actually, individuals have comparatively little need of the formal sources because the informal sources are adequate and often more convenient. Employees frequently go around their bosses or to any place in the organization they wish in order to obtain the information they seek.

Individual and Organizational Relationships

Individuals in a coordinative organization can usually be depended on to accomplish the goals to which they are committed, but they will probably do so in their own way—which may be quite unpredictable. Generally, individuals seeking advancement within the coordinative structure do not concern themselves with rules or norms, nor do they seek insights from others. Instead, they tend to acquire knowledge and insight from their own learning experiences. They are highly adaptable to changes both inside and outside their own group or organization.

Conflict is treated openly and constructively in the coordinative structure. When there is disagreement on a point, those concerned are encouraged not to express their emotions but to deal openly and objectively with the points of the conflict so that the problem may be solved. In fact, it is believed that the resolution of conflict leads to greater cooperation and higher productivity from those involved. Members of the organization are encouraged to stand up and face their problems squarely, whether those problems concern other people, materiel, procedures, or policies.

Information sharing is encouraged, which tends to keep all personnel well informed. The open and aboveboard nature of the system tends to increase trust, since information is free-flowing and no one has to have an "in" to get information about opportunities for advancement.

Individuals in a coordinative organization tend to stick with their particular technology. If they find themselves drifting away from their field of interest they may seek out new jobs or departments—or they may go to a new company in order to stay with their technology.

ANALYZING YOUR OWN ORGANIZATION

In this chapter we have studied how staffing practices differ among the bureaucratic, collaborative, and coordinative organizations so far as their authority paths and decision processes, information flow and information systems, and individual and organizational relationships are concerned. We have already suggested that there are no hard and fast connections between our definitions and the actual staffing practices of the three types of organizations (that is, that there is plenty of room for variation within each type), but we believe that those definitions do set forth a way for you to analyze your own organization.

Two sets of worksheets are provided on the following pages. The first of these is filled out with a sample evaluation which is drawn from the author's own experience; the second is blank, so that you may use it in your own evaluation. When you have completed the worksheet you will be able to see about where your organization stands in relation to the bureaucratic, collaborative, and coordinative structures. Later on we hope to bring this information together with other information you will have developed and use it to help you diagnose and perhaps change the developmental processes of your own organization.

Management development evaluation form
Staffing: authority paths and decision processes

In each of the following sections pick the descriptive statement that most nearly describes your own organization. Make notations of differences.

Organizational practices	Circle one	Notation of where your organization differs
Section I		The decision was mine. I like to get opinions of other department heads who have worked with the person, but I seldom ask his or her peers.
1. Manager alone recommends individual for promotion.	1	
2. Recommendations of other managers and peers influence selection of individual.	②	
3. Individual recommends self.	3	
Section II		I made the final decision but always tried to hear the individual viewpoint. If the person sounded like he or she wasn't interested in the job, I pointed out what turning the job down might mean to future promotions.
1. Final selection decision made at high level in organization—individual usually can't reject.	1	
2. Final selection decision made by hiring manager—individual opinions respected.	②	
3. Final decision made by hiring manager—rejection treated like outside labor market.	3	

Organizational practices	Circle one	Notation of where your organization differs
Section III		We moved people around from all over the company. This was company policy to transfer them broadly.
1. Promotion within immediate organization unit only.	1	
2. Promotion within immediate organization unit and functional specialty.	2	
3. Promotion throughout organization in any functional specialty.	③	
Section IV		Our system was very complex.
1. Simple, direct policies and procedures to control staffing.	1	
2. Complex data-based system.	②	
3. Broad general policies, simplified procedures.	3	
Section V		

Management development evaluation form
Staffing: information flow and information systems

In each of the following sections pick the descriptive statement that most nearly describes your own organization. Make notations of differences.

Organizational practices	Circle one	Notation of where your organization differs
Section I		Managers were required to list openings with Personnel in order to tap into the manpower inventory system. However, managers usually talked to other department heads to find the talent they needed if they didn't have someone in their own department.
1. Manager keeps own record of talented individuals.	1	
2. Manager refers opening to personnel department and "scouts" other departments plus own department for talent.	②	
3. Manager informs personnel department, who post job opening.	3	
Section II		Things were kept secret until the person we wanted was identified. Then we had a discussion with that person to sell him or her on the job.
1. Individual generally unaware of job openings throughout organization.	①	
2. Individual informed of departmental openings but not organizational.	2	
3. Individual informed of all openings throughout the organization.	3	

Organizational practices	Circle one	Notation of where your organization differs
Section III 1. No formal informational system on manpower resources. 2. Well-designed manpower data bank system open to managers only 3. Well-designed manpower data bank system open to all individuals seeking information.	1 ② 3	The company uses a fancy computer-based manpower inventory system. It told me all about the men and women with the talent currently available in the company.
Section IV 1. Individual cannot seek information about job without superior's approval. 2. Individual can seek information from others in department but must have manager's approval to go outside dept. 3. Individual can seek information anywhere in organization.	① 2 3	The rule was no one steps outside of my department without my O.K.— no exceptions.
Section V		

Management development evaluation form
Staffing: individual and organizational relationships

In each of the following sections pick the descriptive statement that most nearly describes your own organization. Make notations of differences.

Organizational practices	Circle one	Notation of where your organization differs
Section I		*Company goals are always first. We listened to the individual's viewpoint, and this helped get his or her support.*
1. Organizational goals first and individual goals not important equals conflict and limited cooperation.	1	
2. Organizational goals primary; individual allowed to express personal goals. Conflict still present but some increase in cooperation.	(2)	
3. Individual goals primary, organization goals matched to the individual equals low conflict, high cooperation.	3	
Section II		*We believe in competition but discourage playing politics — although we know it exists.*
1. High degree of competition for jobs means that playing politics is not unusual.	(1)	
2. Low competition; best-liked, most human person gets job.	2	
3. High competition between qualified persons; most competent gets job.	3	

Organizational practices	Circle one	Notation of where your organization differs
Section III 1. Low trust in staffing decisions (i.e. the best person will get the job—boss's choice wins). 2. Low trust in objectivity of staffing decisions (i.e., best liked wins, but not always most talented). 3. High trust in staffing decisions (i.e., best and most interested person wins).	1 ② 3	Hard to answer this one — how my viewpoint is looking up for my own promotion. I'd say I really have some questions about the objectivity of our system.
Section IV 1. Most loyal person gets job. 2. Longest service, best acquainted person gets job. 3. Loyalty and length of service not a factor in getting job.	1 2 ③	It may not always be true, but we strive for this, particularly in our newer installation.
Section V 1. Managers counsel subordinates on their career. 2. Manager, peers, and personnel counsel individuals in their career. 3. Career counselling available from multiple sources. Main source is how person feels about how he or she fits the job.	① 2 3	This is part of my job. It's actually written into my job description and I've been trained to help individuals get on and stay on the company's career-path plan.

Management development evaluation summary and scores

Add up the numbers you have circled on each of the preceding sheets. Enter the totals in the space provided below, then add them up to get the overall total.

Authority paths and decision processes _____9_____

Information flow and information systems _____6_____

Individual and organizational relationships _____9_____

Total _____24_____

Next, record the total on the following scale. This will give you an indication of where your organization stands on this process in relation to the bureaucratic, collaborative, and coordinative organizations.

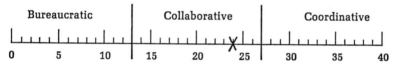

Observations and comments:

Now make your own evaluation on the pages that follow.

Management development evaluation form
Staffing: authority paths and decision processes

In each of the following sections pick the descriptive statement that most nearly describes your own organization. Make notations of differences.

Organizational practices	Circle one	Notation of where your organization differs
Section I		
1. Manager alone recommends individual for promotion.	1	
2. Recommendations of other managers and peers influence selection of individual.	2	
3. Individual recommends self.	3	
Section II		
1. Final selection decision made at high level in organization—individual usually can't reject.	1	
2. Final selection decision made by hiring manager—individual opinions respected.	2	
3. Final decision made by hiring manager—rejection treated like outside labor market.	3	

Organizational practices	Circle one	Notation of where your organization differs
Section III		
1. Promotion within immediate organization unit only.	1	
2. Promotion within immediate organization unit and functional specialty.	2	
3. Promotion throughout organization in any functional specialty.	3	
Section IV		
1. Simple, direct policies and procedures to control staffing.	1	
2. Complex data-based system.	2	
3. Broad general policies, simplified procedures.	3	
Section V		

Management development evaluation form
Staffing: information flow and information systems

In each of the following sections pick the descriptive statement that most nearly describes your own organization. Make notations of differences.

Organizational practices	Circle one	Notation of where your organization differs
Section I		
1. Manager keeps own record of talented individuals.	1	
2. Manager refers opening to personnel department and "scouts" other departments plus own department for talent.	2	
3. Manager informs personnel department, who post job opening.	3	
Section II		
1. Individual generally unaware of job openings throughout organization.	1	
2. Individual informed of departmental openings but not organizational.	2	
3. Individual informed of all openings throughout the organization.	3	

Organizational practices	Circle one	Notation of where your organization differs
Section III		
1. No formal informational system on manpower resources.	1	
2. Well-designed manpower data bank system open to managers only	2	
3. Well-designed manpower data bank system open to all individuals seeking information.	3	
Section IV		
1. Individual cannot seek information about job without superior's approval.	1	
2. Individual can seek information from others in department but must have manager's approval to go outside dept.	2	
3. Individual can seek information anywhere in organization.	3	
Section V		

Management development evaluation form
Staffing: individual and organizational relationships

In each of the following sections pick the descriptive statement that most nearly describes your own organization. Make notations of differences.

Organizational practices	Circle one	Notation of where your organization differs
Section I		
1. Organizational goals first and individual goals not important equals conflict and limited cooperation.	1	
2. Organizational goals primary; individual allowed to express personal goals. Conflict still present but some increase in cooperation.	2	
3. Individual goals primary, organization goals matched to the individual equals low conflict, high cooperation.	3	
Section II		
1. High degree of competition for jobs means that playing politics is not unusual.	1	
2. Low competition; best-liked, most human person gets job.	2	
3. High competition between qualified persons; most competent gets job.	3	

Organizational practices	Circle one	Notation of where your organization differs
Section III		
1. Low trust in staffing decisions (i.e. the best person will get the job—boss's choice wins).	1	
2. Low trust in objectivity of staffing decisions (i.e., best liked wins, but not always most talented).	2	
3. High trust in staffing decisions (i.e., best and most interested person wins).	3	
Section IV		
1. Most loyal person gets job.	1	
2. Longest service, best acquainted person gets job.	2	
3. Loyalty and length of service not a factor in getting job.	3	
Section V		
1. Managers counsel subordinates on their career.	1	
2. Manager, peers, and personnel counsel individuals in their career.	2	
3. Career counselling available from multiple sources. Main source is how person feels about how he or she fits the job.	3	

Management development evaluation summary and scores

Add up the numbers you have circled on each of the preceding sheets. Enter the totals in the space provided below, then add them up to get the overall total.

Authority paths and decision processes   _____

Information flow and information systems   _____

Individual and organizational relationships   _____

                                Total   _____

Next, record the total on the following scale. This will give you an indication of where your organization stands on this process in relation to the bureaucratic, collaborative, and coordinative organizations.

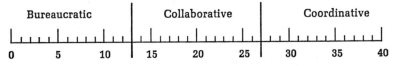

Observations and comments:

6/Goal-Setting Processes

The goal-setting process, or definition of what is expected of an individual in an organization, is considered one of the imperatives for successful development of managers within the organizational context. In this chapter we will examine the nature of the goal-setting processes as they are likely to be found within the three basic organizational structures: bureaucratic, collaborative, and coordinative. This chapter is designed to examine goal-setting processes as they relate to authority paths and decision processes, information flow and information systems, and individual and organizational relationships. Essentially, we will follow the same format followed in Chapter 5.

We previously explained the goal-setting process in terms of who makes the decisions relative to the goal toward which the individual is working. On the one hand, under the bureaucratic structure the goals are preset and determined by the higher authorities within the organization. On the other hand, in a coordinative system, the goals are usually set by the individual.

BUREAUCRATIC STRUCTURE

Authority Paths and Decision Processes

The goal-setting process frequently found within the bureaucratic structure can be seen in the predetermined and imposed quotas, production standards, and performance goals. Such quotas and standards are largely determined by the manager (though they often originate at higher levels) and are usually imposed on the individual, who is expected to meet them. Oftentimes the standards are set by a third party, such as industrial engineering, time-study, or possibly a personnel group. Such goals are serial in nature. That is, each person's work is closely linked with the operation preceding and the operation following his or her job—much like the work on an assembly line. When one person fails to meet the goal, those who are to perform subsequent operations also fall behind. Another characteristic of this type of goal-setting process is its lack of flexibility; it does not adapt well to major schedule changes except where those changes have been anticipated and procedures prepared in advance. This means that when unanticipated changes or breakdowns occur, emergency handling procedures are necessary.

Information Flow and Information Systems

In the bureaucratic structure, information systems in general and the flow of information in particular run from the top down. Goals are set primarily by officials at the top and are gradually processed down through the organization to lower levels. As the information filters down, the individual progressively has less and less responsibility for initiating and influencing information. By the time it reaches the bottom of the organization, the individual is expected to follow out instructions to the letter. Generally, an individual in this case will be told by his or her boss to zero in on a very specific portion of an overall target and not to worry about others and how they accomplish their work. There is no information about why the job is important or what progress others are making in their work. In this situation, there is very little upward flow of information and feedback relative to the validity of the targets. Furthermore, individual suggestions and contributions are nil.

There are generally no formal procedures involved in passing information down through the organization in this manner except through such control systems as production scheduling, order processing, financial reports, etc.

Individual and Organizational Relationships

As previously mentioned, individuals in a bureaucratic structure are assigned goals with no explanation of how their work affects that of other people. They may not understand why a particular goal was set the way it was, and they may in fact perceive management's goals as incompatible with their own.

Their behavior is predictable: Having little in common with management, individuals are seldom interested in the interdependency between their jobs and others in the organization. They see themselves as unimportant to the organization, and so tend to do only what they have to do and no more. They do not contribute ideas or suggestions for upgrading production or manufacturing processes or for improving their own or the company's goals. They have been conditioned over the years to accept the fact that they are not going to be involved in determining what they do, so they have become passive, much like robots—part of the organization's mechanical processes.

COLLABORATIVE STRUCTURE

Authority Paths and Decision Processes

In collaborative organizations, although quotas may still be used, the goal-setting process is conducted on a mutual basis. The group members get together and agree on their goals in conjunction with a third party such as the Industrial Engineering Department. In setting goals of this type, the relationship between group and individual goals is taken into consideration. For example, the group has a goal, and each individual has a subgoal; the emphasis tends to be on the group goal, but if an individual falls behind in his or her subgoal schedule, other members of the group will jump in to help.

Goals may or may not be serial in nature. Each individual may handle a complete product or project right through to the end, depending on no one else for either preceding or subsequent stages. Interdependency between individuals is much less important in the collaborative structure than in the bureaucratic structure.

Under a collaborative structure the targets are adjustable; however, they cannot be classified as "highly flexible." They are adjusted as the group and total organization see a need for change.

Information Flow and Information Systems

In a collaborative organization the overall goals are set at the top of the organization. However, the individuals down in the organization are given some options in making decisions relative to these goals. Because group processes prevail in the goal-setting process, groups are given information essential to their operations, but they are not given information relative to other operations within the organization. There tends to be some upward-flow of information within each group, and there is generally a limited amount beyond the unit. There are fairly well defined formal procedures set up for this type of system, particularly relating to such things as profit centers, budgeting procedures, and scheduling of work. In order to accomplish their work, individuals are given essential information relative to their own unit's operations.

Individual and Organizational Relationships

In a collaborative organization an individual's goals are frequently congruent with the goals of other individuals. They may not be the same, but they are compatible in the sense that both sets of goals work together to strengthen the organization. On the other hand, it is not uncommon for the goals of one unit within an organization to conflict with the goals of another unit, or for one unit to be doing work which in some ways contradicts the work of another unit. Individuals in this type of organization have a strong commitment to the group goals and generally a relatively lower commitment toward the broader organizational goals. They have an interdependent and cooperative relationship which is recognized by each individual within the group. Just as with a squad of soldiers with high morale, you will find the group members cooperating and working together in a helping way to assure that the group's goals are accomplished, for like the squad, the group members have a collaborative and helping spirit. The group can function relatively independently of other units in the organization. This carries its own risks, however, for any group may thus find itself out of step with the other units within the organization.

In a collaborative structure you will see individuals involved in the goal-setting process as this process relates to their own department. They will have very little concern for organizational goals or other units within the organization, but will direct commitment and cooperation primarily toward fellow department workers.

COORDINATIVE STRUCTURE

Authority Paths and Decision Processes

Goals are important in a coordinative structure. They are largely determined by the individual in a coordinative way with other individuals in the department, unit, or total organization.

In determining goals, the individual checks to see how they fit in with others and whether predetermined individual deadlines can be met. Oftentimes the deadlines are determined as a result of the summary of all of the individual goals. These are then compared with the broader commitment made by the unit (department) to other parts of the organization or to outside organizations and the differences are reconciled. Quite often the sum of individual goals adds up to higher standards than those set by the client organization for whom the goals are designed.

Goals toward which an individual works are based on his or her own expertise. It is the individual's own responsibility under such a structure to coordinate such expertise with that of others in the organization. In a coordinative structure the goal-setting process is a highly flexible and fluid process involving numerous changes and a high degree of uncertainty about what a specific goal may be at any particular time.

In summary, goal-setting processes vary from management's setting of rigid standards to a situation where the standards are set by the individual in relationship to other individuals and based on expertise within the organization.

Information Flow and Information Systems

Since the goal-setting process in a coordinative structure is initiated by the individual, each member of that structure needs to have basic information relative to his or her own unit of operation as well as to the organization as a whole. It is, therefore, up to the individual to seek out information relative to the goals of others within his unit and to understand their objectives in relationship to his own. Each person develops this bank of information in terms of the total organization and is assumed, therefore, to be able to make intelligent decisions relative to his or her immediate responsibilties and goals. There is a relatively high level of information sharing both within and between units. You can see how this would take place in an organization where expertise is the basis for decision-making and leadership.

In order for a person in a coordinative organization to do quality work up to his or her potential, he or she must have information about how others are performing their work—their procedures as well as their results. In a coordinative organization, information systems are flexible and designed around the "need-for-information" concept. Information hardware (computers, etc.), plays an important role in speedy information flow, so there is usually a highly sophisticated information bank with information feedback systems providing each individual with data relative to his or her own operation as well as other operations within the organization. There are also numerous informal ways of transmitting information.

In the bureaucratic structure, very little information is shared that top management decides is not necessary, while the coordinative structure provides as much information as the individual feels he or she needs.

Individual and Organizational Relationships

In the coordinative structure, the individual's basic commitment for accomplishing objectives is to himself or herself, and not to the group or the organization. And when one person's goals do not relate to those of other group members or of the group itself, it may seem that there is very little interdependency among individuals. This assumption is valid so long as goals are not related, but when a person sees another member of the group falling behind and realizes that this will have an effect on his or her own goal achievement, then he or she is often willing to give assistance—technical or otherwise—toward the accomplishment of the other's goals. Such help is reciprocated, of course, whenever it is needed. It becomes apparent, therefore, that members of the coordinatively structured group—who at first glance seem so independent of one another—are in fact required to collaborate to a high degree. Various group members who have practically no relationship at all at some times may have very close and active job relationships at other times.

Obviously, a person cannot know how the progress of the other group members will affect his or her own goals without some knowledge of what the other members do and how they do it. Hence the necessity, as mentioned in the preceding section, for each group member to be well informed about the objectives of other group members and the relationship of those objectives to his or her own. Of course, when two (or more) group members do realize that the goals they have been pursuing independently must now be pursued in collaboration with someone else, there is likely to be conflict—of approaches, priorities, etc. But because those group members are well informed and have participated in their own goal-setting, they tend to see rather easily the advantages of and necessity for cooperation. This is not necessarily from any humanitarian attitudes but rather from recognition of the fact that they cannot achieve their goals without giving and receiving that cooperation.

ANALYZING YOUR OWN ORGANIZATION

Just as in Chapter 5, we would like to have you now examine your own organization in terms of the structure which we have described in this chapter—goal-setting processes.

We remind you that it is to your advantage to examine the first four worksheets, which contain a sample evaluation, before starting the evaluation of your own organization.

Management development evaluation form
Goal-setting: authority paths and decision processes

In each of the following sections pick the descriptive statement that most nearly describes your own organization. Make notations of differences.

Organizational practices	Circle one	Notation of where your organization differs
Section I		Goals are set at the top, but they are cut up and distributed to group members.
1. Quotas/production standards set by management.	1	
2. Quotas/performance standards and goals set jointly between management and individual/group.	②	
3. Individual sets own goals in line with group and organizational goals.	3	
Section II		Goals are usually self-standing—i.e., what one person does isn't too dependent on another person.
1. Goals are serial in nature— i.e., each person contributes in series to next person's goals.	1	
2. Individual goals within group may be serial or separate. Group goals serial between groups.	②	
3. Goals are separate and complete. Individual responsible for entire goal accomplishment.	3	

Organizational practices	Circle one	Notation of where your organization differs
Section III 1. Goals are fixed and infrequently changed. 2. Goals are adjusted as the group and situation dictate. 3. Goals are highly flexible and in a continuous state of readjustment.	① 2 3	We never change a target once it's set. The company doesn't believe in changing a goal even if we know we can't make it.
Section IV		
Section V		

Management development evaluation form
Goal-setting: information flow and information systems

In each of the following sections pick the descriptive statement that most
nearly describes your own organization. Make notations of differences.

Organizational practices	Circle one	Notation of where your organization differs
Section I		
1. Goals are set at top of organization and processed to lower levels through organizational channels.	①	*This should be about 1½, since goals, although they come from the top, are in part negotiated with each individual.*
2. Broad goals are set at top, with unit subgoals being set by the group and individuals.	2	
3. Goal-setting process initiated by individual. Individual goals are coordinated into unit and organization-wide goals.	3	
Section II		
1. Small amount of feedback backup in organization to confirm validity of preset goals.	①	*People don't contribute much information to top management unless they are asked.*
2. Cross communication and checking of goals within group. Small amount of confirmation upward in organization.	2	
3. Cross checking and coordination of information at all levels where required for effective performance.	3	

Organizational practices	Circle one	Notation of where your organization differs
Section III 1. No formal information system used. Organization structure provides vehicle for transmission of goal information. 2. Well-developed formal goal-setting system required. 3. Informal and broadly defined goal-setting system.	1 ② 3	System is well-developed. In part it's a computerized program and we are all given reports indicating where we are in terms of our preset goals.
Section IV		
Section V		

Management development evaluation form
Goal-setting: individual and organizational relationships

In each of the following sections pick the descriptive statement that most nearly describes your own organization. Make notations of differences.

Organizational practices	Circle one	Notation of where your organization differs
Section I		
1. Individual's goals often in conflict with organizational goals.	1	*Goals set by the company and department are usually chosen because someone higher up believes they're Right for Everyone.*
2. Individual goals often in agreement with group goals but not necessarily organization goals.	②	
3. Individual goals considered primary and are combined to form group and organizational goals.	3	
Section II		
1. Limited individual commitment toward assigned goals.	①	*Because they are mostly assigned goals, people do what's expected — but it doesn't mean they like it.*
2. High commitment to group goals but not necessarily organizational goals.	2	
3. High commitment to individual's own goals.	3	

Organizational practices	Circle one	Notation of where your organization differs
Section III		In general, individuals see how the assigned goals fit the overall picture.
1. Individual usually fails to see inter-dependent (serial nature) of his goals as related to others.	1	
2. Individual recognizes inter-dependent relationship of his goal achievement to others in group but not the total organization.	②	
3. Interdependence of individual goals with group and organizational goals is understood.	3	
Section IV		Since goals are mostly predetermined, people only need follow-up and implementing skills.
1. Skill in setting goals not required.	①	
2. Skill in group processes (collaborative skills) used to set goals is required.	2	
3. Goal-setting and coordinative skills required.	3	
Section V		

Management development evaluation summary and scores

Add up the numbers you have circled on each of the preceding sheets. Enter the totals in the space provided below, then add them up to get the overall total.

Authority paths and decision processes   _5_

Information flow and information systems   _4_

Individual and organizational relationships   _6_

                                 Total   _15_

Next, record the total on the following scale. This will give you an indication of where your organization stands on this process in relation to the bureaucratic, collaborative, and coordinative organizations.

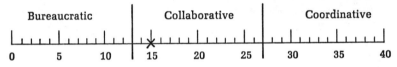

Observations and comments:

Now make your own evaluation on the pages that follow.

Management development evaluation form
Goal-setting: authority paths and decision processes

In each of the following sections pick the descriptive statement that most nearly describes your own organization. Make notations of differences.

Organizational practices	Circle one	Notation of where your organization differs
Section I		
1. Quotas/production standards set by management.	1	
2. Quotas/performance standards and goals set jointly between management and individual/group.	2	
3. Individual sets own goals in line with group and organizational goals.	3	
Section II		
1. Goals are serial in nature— i.e., each person contributes in series to next person's goals.	1	
2. Individual goals within group may be serial or separate. Group goals serial between groups.	2	
3. Goals are separate and complete. Individual responsible for entire goal accomplishment.	3	

Organizational practices	Circle one	Notation of where your organization differs
Section III		
1. Goals are fixed and infrequently changed.	1	
2. Goals are adjusted as the group and situation dictate.	2	
3. Goals are highly flexible and in a continuous state of readjustment.	3	
Section IV		
Section V		

Management development evaluation form
Goal-setting: information flow and information systems

In each of the following sections pick the descriptive statement that most nearly describes your own organization. Make notations of differences.

Organizational practices	Circle one	Notation of where your organization differs
Section I		
1. Goals are set at top of organization and processed to lower levels through organizational channels.	1	
2. Broad goals are set at top, with unit subgoals being set by the group and individuals.	2	
3. Goal-setting process initiated by individual. Individual goals are coordinated into unit and organization-wide goals.	3	
Section II		
1. Small amount of feedback backup in organization to confirm validity of preset goals.	1	
2. Cross communication and checking of goals within group. Small amount of confirmation upward in organization.	2	
3. Cross checking and coordination of information at all levels where required for effective performance.	3	

Organizational practices	Circle one	Notation of where your organization differs
Section III		
1. No formal information system used. Organization structure provides vehicle for transmission of goal information.	1	
2. Well-developed formal goal-setting system required.	2	
3. Informal and broadly defined goal-setting system.	3	
Section IV		
Section V		

Management development evaluation form
Goal-setting: individual and organizational relationships

In each of the following sections pick the descriptive statement that most nearly describes your own organization. Make notations of differences.

Organizational practices	Circle one	Notation of where your organization differs
Section I		
1. Individual's goals often in conflict with organizational goals.	1	
2. Individual goals often in agreement with group goals but not necessarily organization goals.	2	
3. Individual goals considered primary and are combined to form group and organizational goals.	3	
Section II		
1. Limited individual commitment toward assigned goals.	1	
2. High commitment to group goals but not necessarily organizational goals.	2	
3. High commitment to individual's own goals.	3	

Organizational practices	Circle one	Notation of where your organization differs
Section III		
1. Individual usually fails to see inter-dependent (serial nature) of his goals as related to others.	1	
2. Individual recognizes inter-dependent relationship of his goal achievement to others in group but not the total organization.	2	
3. Interdependence of individual goals with group and organizational goals is understood.	3	
Section IV		
1. Skill in setting goals not required.	1	
2. Skill in group processes (collaborative skills) used to set goals is required.	2	
3. Goal-setting and coordinative skills required.	3	
Section V		

Management development evaluation summary and scores

Add up the numbers you have circled on each of the preceding sheets. Enter the totals in the space provided below, then add them up to get the overall total.

Authority paths and decision processes   ———

Information flow and information systems   ———

Individual and organizational relationships   ———

Total   ———

Next, record the total on the following scale. This will give you an indication of where your organization stands on this process in relation to the bureaucratic, collaborative, and coordinative organizations.

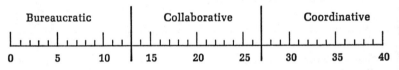

Observations and comments:

7/Work-Performance Processes

We have considered staffing practices and the goal-setting process as major factors in the managerial development process.
The third contributing factor is that of the performance of the
work itself, or how the work is done and what this does to
stimulate managerial development. In this chapter we will examine the various characteristics of work performance in terms
of authority paths and decision processes, information flow and
information systems, and individual and organizational relationships for the three forms of organizations: bureaucratic, collaborative, and coordinative.

Let us remind you again that we are examining these various
characteristics as they relate to operational organizations so
that a critical evaluation can be made of your own organization.
The hoped-for conclusion is that you will be able to better understand your own organization and the processes that affect
the development of managers.

For our purposes we will talk about the *scope of the work*
being performed; that is, its extent and degree of specialization
as well as the degree of freedom that the individual has in deciding how he or she is going to do the job.

BUREAUCRATIC STRUCTURE

Authority Paths and Decision Processes

The work assigned to an individual in a bureaucratic structure is highly structured and procedurally laid out. It involves
a step-by-step description of precisely how the job is to be performed. At the extreme (production operation) it describes the
actual operation of equipment, the placing of materials, and
even goes so far as to define the exact hand movement. It
focuses on the narrowness of the function and the preciseness
of the operation, leaving little or no opportunity for original or
creative thinking on the part of the operator. Anytime an operational change is to be made, the operator must first check carefully with the higher authority responsible for the design of the
work and for redefinition of the job.

Work of this type is usually of a serial nature, that is, jobs are
in sequence with other jobs. The satisfactory completion of one
job is highly dependent on another. If the employee's job is

completed according to specification, it is then possible for the next person in line to complete his or her work.

Applying this approach to a salaried or management level position, it has been referred to as functional specialization. Where an individual is highly specialized in conducting a very specific task within the organization, such as posting to a ledger, correcting mathematical errors in insurance claims, performing a highly sophisticated scientific test etc., all such tasks would be predetermined by some outside group or person.

Information Flow and Information Systems

In a bureaucratic structure you will find that the procedures for information dissemination are well-established and involve a high degree of central control within the organization. One of the problems of such control, however, is that it allows the company to give the employee only that information which is essential to the performance of the job itself (the work-related or job-related information). Bureaucratic structures strive to conceal or hold back information which is not related to the job. The employee in this type of operation frequently strives to obtain more information; if he or she succeeds, it is only through the informal structure of the organization.

In the bureaucratic situation, the information flow on work procedures is primarily downward, with relatively little or no information flow upward. This means that the individual employee holds back and does not offer constructive suggestions on how the work might be performed more efficiently. It seems to the worker that any improvement in work techniques will benefit only the company, and so he or she is unwilling to share such information without being "bribed" or otherwise enticed.

Individual and Organizational Relationships

Individual behavior in the bureaucratic structure is *highly predictable* and generally not very cooperative. People in a bureaucratic structure do tend to follow the rules in order to survive, but there is relatively little seeking out of information to clarify responsibilities. Information relative to the work situation is often distorted to fit one's own personal needs. Individuals deviating from prescribed policies or work practices are held accountable for the deviation and disciplined accordingly. Those who are unable to adapt to the high degree of structure withdraw, become passive, or even leave the structure entirely. The relationships between the individual and the bureaucratic organization are frequently conflicting. That is, there tends to be a high degree of conflict between the individual's own personal objectives, wishes, and needs and the objectives, wishes, and needs of the organization as a whole. The organization insists that its personnel repress *their* objectives and needs and direct their energy and efforts toward the organizational goals. The conflict is most easily seen in the relationship between union and management, where the organizational goals are described as being primarily economic and the union's goals are described as being primarily personal or human. Conflict between these two highly structured power bases—the management power base and the union power bases —often must be resolved by a third-party negotiator. Resolution and/or neutralization of differences is seldom accomplished—or is accomplished with great difficulty— due to the high degree of polarization involved.

Bureaucratic management considers it improper for a conflict between two people to arise; therefore, such conflict is discouraged and the individuals involved are reprimanded or sanctioned for their behavior. Yet conflicts are likely to occur when an individual feels no responsibility toward others (as is the case in the bureaucratic structure) but only toward himself or herself. After all, the individual in this structure is interested primarily in self-preservation, not cooperation. In fact, bureaucratic structures show a relatively low order of cooperation except in maintaining safe practices, for example, or in emergencies. Where personal safety is concerned, or an emergency arises, the level of cooperation is high and the level of conflict low.

COLLABORATIVE STRUCTURE

Authority Paths and Decision Processes

In a collaborative structure, the way a job is to be performed is usually precisely defined in a job description. The difference between the collaborative and bureaucratic structures on this point is that the group in which the individual works has a high degree of influence on the way the job is designed as well as on changes that are made in the job. Although the group can influence the change and redesign of the job, the final approval of changes must come from high authorities within the organization.

In a collaborative structure it is not uncommon to find a serial flow of material and processes within a specific group. However, it is more common to find small groups or teams of people working together in a sharing and cooperative way, allowing individuals to perform various operations according to their skill and competency.

Information Flow and Information Systems

Because of the group orientation so typical in a collaborative structure, information which may be useful to the group is generally shared with all members of the group—even though it may be directly applicable to only one group member. The implication is that the group will function better if all the members know everything that is relevant to the group. Likewise, it is common for individuals to freely share their ideas and suggestions with other group members. There is some tendency for information to flow outward in this type of organization, but generally there is very little exchange between one group and another.

There are usually well-developed control systems at the group level that are designed to assure quality, quantity, and various other types of results.

Individual and Organizational Relationships

In a collaborative structure, just as in a bureaucratic structure, behavior is *highly predictable;* that is, people follow the generally prescribed approaches to solving problems in conducting their work. Yet, as has been mentioned, there is more sharing of information within the group itself. There is apt to be a fairly high level of cooperation and a low level of conflict between group members. The nature of the collaborative structure is such that in order to accomplish their work, individuals become highly committed to supportive behavior, which tends to foster cooperative relationships and reduces conflict. Conflict in such cases is usually dealt with openly within the group itself.

In this type of structure there is a general feeling of responsibility to other members of the group directed at accomplishing the assigned tasks. Information and solutions to problems are usually sought within the work team and seldom shared outside. A person probably will not feel commitment to members of other groups unless he or she can expect to obtain some personal or group benefit in return.

Conflict between groups is most often suppressed by the group members, and there is apt to be a fairly high degree of polarization between the employees' point of view and management's point of view.

COORDINATIVE STRUCTURE

Authority Paths and Decision Processes

The conditions of the coordinative structure are much different from those of the bureaucratic and collaborative structures. In the coordinative structure the individual is given the broad framework of the job and then allowed the freedom to complete the job as he or she wishes. Details are left up to the worker, who can change relationships with other people, devise new techniques or procedures, and so on. The only conditions are that the job must be completed by the time, within the cost, and to the specifications given by the organization. Generally speaking, this type of operation involves the total task; that is, completion of the total assembly or entire project.

Information Flow and Information Systems

Within the coordinative structure, individuals share information where it is essential that they do so in order to accomplish their tasks. They look to the person with the expertise and there is in most instances an open, free sharing of information. There is, as a rule, no interference by other individuals, whatever their level of authority. In a coordinative structure it is most common to see communication systems used to the maximum, with computers, television information relay systems, and other techniques all freely providing the individual with information which he or she feels is necessary for the accomplishment of the job. What one person feels is necessary may not be the same to another, but there are no value judgments placed on this by organizational authorities. It is essentially left up to the individual.

Individual and Organizational Relationships

In the coordinative structure the way in which an individual will perform a given task is *highly unpredictable*. The results, however, are predictable. As we have already said, the techniques are up to the individual, so long as the results are satisfactory to the organization. There tends to be a moderately high level of conflict in a coordinative structure. This conflict is considered to be normal and is confronted openly, with no attempt to suppress it. In fact, conflict is believed to be healthy in that it stimulates increased innovation and productivity. The one requirement of any coordinative structure is that conflict be dealt with openly and resolved in some way.

Individuals and groups in a coordinative structure tend to cooperate and share technical information and resources only as the job requires. When that requirement is low, so is the contact between both individuals and groups. But when the solving of a problem or the completion of a job make it necessary, cooperation between individuals and/or groups reaches a very high level. The organization's members are aware that they— and the groups they make up—are dependent on one another, and they recognize the benefits of providing mutual cooperation when it is needed.

ANALYZING YOUR OWN ORGANIZATION

As we've done in Chapters 5 and 6, we are now going to give you an opportunity to examine your own organization in terms of the three structures which we have described. The illustration which precedes the worksheets will give you some sense of how to apply the work performance processes for your own organization.

Management development evaluation form
Work performance: authority paths and decision processes

In each of the following sections pick the descriptive statement that most nearly describes your own organization. Make notations of differences.

Organizational practices	Circle one	Notation of where your organization differs
Section I		
1. Specific step-by-step "how-to" job description (narrow functions).	1	*Work is defined in general terms. The employee is allowed to vary within a broad definition.*
2. Specific how-to job descriptions.	2	
3. Broad key areas of responsibility—individual decides specifics.	③	
Section II		
1. Changes made by higher authority.	1	*The individual can define changes but must check with his or her boss.*
2. Group can make changes subject to higher authority's OK.	②	
3. Individual makes changes within broad limits, i.e., relates to others' goals.	3	

Organizational practices	Circle one	Notation of where your organization differs
Section III		Work is done by groups sometimes in serial flow, sometimes independent — depending on the situation.
1. Serial flow of work.	1	
2. Serial or small total task accomplishment.	(2)	
3. Total task accomplishment based on expertise.	3	
Section IV		
Section V		

Management development evaluation form
Work performance: information flow and information systems

In each of the following sections pick the descriptive statement that most
nearly describes your own organization. Make notations of differences.

Organizational practices	Circle one	Notation of where your organization differs
Section I		You get information related to your job, but even here you may have to generate data yourself (i.e., collect information yourself).
1. Only work-related information needed for individual to get the job done is provided.	1	
2. Group information shared with those accountable for results.	(2)	
3. Individual shares information with those who need it.	3	
Section II		Very competitive situation. Fear that giving someone an idea will result in their getting ahead of you.
1. Individual does not offer constructive suggestions.	(1)	
2. Sharing of ideas within group.	2	
3. Individual ideas are openly offered.	3	

Organizational practices	Circle one	Notation of where your organization differs
Section III		Information is used to control and check progress of work and results produced.
1. Well-developed control systems.	(1)	
2. Well-developed control system at unit level as well as top.	2	
3. Full use of latest communication ideas to facilitate information flow.	3	
Section IV		
Section V		

Management development evaluation form
Work performance: individual and organizational relationships

In each of the following sections pick the descriptive statement that most nearly describes your own organization. Make notations of differences.

Organizational practices	Circle one	Notation of where your organization differs
Section I		*Someone getting into conflict with another person is told to "cool it." No resolution, just suppression.*
1. Conflict between persons suppressed, negotiated by third party.	①	
2. Intragroup conflict dealt with, intergroup conflict suppressed.	2	
3. Conflict throughout organization confronted and resolved.	3	
Section II		*Fairly high degree of cooperation with small work groups.*
1. Cooperation limited to emergencies.	1	
2. Intergroup cooperation high.	②	
3. High level of trust.		

Organizational practices	Circle one	Notation of where your organization differs
Section III	(1)	*Little feeling of need to help others attitude is, "I had to learn, so let him learn for himself."*
1. Individuals don't feel responsibility.		
2. Individuals feel responsible for each other within group.	2	
3. Feeling of responsibility to others for individual contributions.	3	
Section IV		
Section V		

Management development evaluation summary and scores

Add up the numbers you have circled on each of the preceding sheets. Enter the totals in the space provided below, then add them up to get the overall total.

Authority paths and decision processes	_7_
Information flow and information systems	_4_
Individual and organizational relationships	_4_
Total	_15_

Next, record the total on the following scale. This will give you an indication of where your organization stands on this process in relation to the bureaucratic, collaborative, and coordinative organizations.

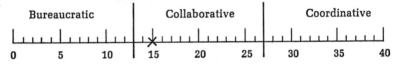

Observations and comments:

Now make your own evaluation on the pages that follow.

Management development evaluation form
Work performance: authority paths and decision processes

In each of the following sections pick the descriptive statement that most nearly describes your own organization. Make notations of differences.

Organizational practices	Circle one	Notation of where your organization differs
Section I		
1. Specific step-by-step "how-to" job description (narrow functions).	1	
2. Specific how-to job descriptions.	2	
3. Broad key areas of responsibility—individual decides specifics.	3	
Section II		
1. Changes made by higher authority.	1	
2. Group can make changes subject to higher authority's OK.	2	
3. Individual makes changes within broad limits, i.e., relates to others' goals.	3	

Organizational practices	Circle one	Notation of where your organization differs
Section III		
1. Serial flow of work.	1	
2. Serial or small total task accomplishment.	2	
3. Total task accomplishment based on expertise.	3	
Section IV		
Section V		

Management development evaluation form
Work performance: information flow and information systems

In each of the following sections pick the descriptive statement that most nearly describes your own organization. Make notations of differences.

Organizational practices	Circle one	Notation of where your organization differs
Section I		
1. Only work-related information needed for individual to get the job done is provided.	1	
2. Group information shared with those accountable for results.	2	
3. Individual shares information with those who need it.	3	
Section II		
1. Individual does not offer constructive suggestions.	1	
2. Sharing of ideas within group.	2	
3. Individual ideas are openly offered.	3	

Organizational practices	Circle one	Notation of where your organization differs
Section III		
1. Well-developed control systems.	1	
2. Well-developed control system at unit level as well as top.	2	
3. Full use of latest communication ideas to facilitate information flow.	3	
Section IV		
Section V		

Management development evaluation form
Work performance: individual and organizational relationships

In each of the following sections pick the descriptive statement that most nearly describes your own organization. Make notations of differences.

Organizational practices	Circle one	Notation of where your organization differs
Section I		
1. Conflict between persons suppressed, negotiated by third party.	1	
2. Intragroup conflict dealt with, intergroup conflict suppressed.	2	
3. Conflict throughout organization confronted and resolved.	3	
Section II		
1. Cooperation limited to emergencies.	1	
2. Intergroup cooperation high.	2	
3. High level of trust.		

Organizational practices	Circle one	Notation of where your organization differs
Section III	1	
1. Individuals don't feel responsibility.		
2. Individuals feel responsible for each other within group.	2	
3. Feeling of responsibility to others for individual contributions.	3	
Section IV		
Section V		

Management development evaluation summary and scores

Add up the numbers you have circled on each of the preceding sheets. Enter the totals in the space provided below, then add them up to get the overall total.

Authority paths and decision processes   _____

Information flow and information systems   _____

Individual and organizational relationships   _____

                                          Total   _____

Next, record the total on the following scale. This will give you an indication of where your organization stands on this process in relation to the bureaucratic, collaborative, and coordinative organizations.

Bureaucratic	Collaborative	Coordinative
0 5 10	15 20 25	30 35 40

Observations and comments:

8/Evaluation Processes

The last job-related process we want to examine, as it relates to how managers develop, is the evaluation process; that is, how individual performance results are evaluated. The focus here is primarily on how individuals obtain information concerning the effectiveness with which they are performing their work and how they measure and adjust their performance inputs. On the one hand their bosses may be making subjective, judgmental decisions relative to their performance; on the other hand, each individual may be making judgments about his or her own performance.

Although it is impossible to assign an exact value, we believe that the evaluation process itself represents one of the most important factors contributing to the development of the manager.

We will examine the evaluation process as we have in the other three job-related processes, by looking at the three mediating organizational factors in terms of the three structures, bureaucratic, collaborative, and coordinative.

BUREAUCRATIC STRUCTURE

Authority Paths and Decision Processes

In a bureaucratic structure, the superior reserves or holds power over the individual due to his or her position in the organization, and makes subjective and evaluative decisions relative to the individual's performance. He or she does this on a day-to-day basis and frequently uses formal evaluation procedures set forth by the organization. For the most part, though, such procedures follow a highly subjective evaluation based principally on the attitude of the boss toward the subordinate. It is not uncommon in a bureaucratic structure to find no formal evaluation procedure. In such cases evaluations tend to be informal, where a boss makes spontaneous judgments involving yes-or-no types of decision relative to the individual.

In the bureaucratic type of structure, the feedback of work performance is not directed to the individual performing the job, but rather to his or her manager or a higher authority. The manager then takes this information, interprets it, and sifts out those pieces of information that he or she wishes to deal with directly as they relate to the individual.

Information Flow and Information Systems

Information flow in relationship to the evaluation processes is closely linked. We would like to be clear that we believe information can move in various directions (upward as well as downward, and horizontally), and that the way information flows has a major impact on how effectively processes function for the individual.

In a bureaucratic structure, information feedback is indirect. The individual performs a job and produces certain kinds of results; these results are measured by a second person, who reports on them to the worker's superior. The superior feeds back this information to the individual. To take an example from a production situation: A worker turns out a product which is later examined by an inspector down the line. The inspector makes out a report and sends it to the worker's foreman. The foreman gives feedback directly to the worker on how he or she is doing. One trouble with this type of feedback is that it tends to be highly authoritarian in nature and, in most instances, is critical rather than complimentary. It tends to be personality-oriented, in that the identification of poor performance is apt to be associated with those things the manager believes are negative qualities, such as bad attitude, poor relationships with other people, etc. It also may not suggest what the worker should do in order to overcome his or her problems (there may or may not be a formal procedure for suggesting this). Therefore, the information which the individual receives is usually highly critical, personality-oriented, and diffuse, or unhelpful.

Individual and Organizational Relationships

The evaluation relationships which prevail in a bureaucratic structure require that the manager make judgments or conclusions about the individual. In such cases the manager performs in the capacity of judge, and the accused (the individual) has little recourse but to accept the judge's evaluation. Such a situation tends to foster a high degree of mistrust between subordinate and manager, as well as distrust between peers within the organization. This, in turn, evokes a low degree of loyalty toward the manager as well as a feeling of one-up and one-down relationships. The one-up and one-down relationship has been described as a father-son relationship in which the father decides what's good for his son and the son is required to accept these judgments as gospel. As one might imagine, this stimulates defensive behavior on the part of the individual and a nonconstructive boss/subordinate relationship.

The judgmental character of this evaluation approach causes the individual to feel little ownership in the work he or she performs, to behave defensively, and to avoid responsibility.

It is generally agreed that evaluation is essential to life itself; without receiving feedback we would not be able to survive in our environment. We must have information which tells us how we are performing, where we are in relationship to others, and how we are progressing through time. Thus the evaluation process is highly important to development. The range of behavior, depending on the structural situation, is from a position of defensiveness and resistance (where the superior evaluates the individual) to a self-assessing assertive posture where the individual evaluates himself. In the bureaucratic structure the manager plays God or judge, which reduces ownership and elicits defensive and avoidance behavior, lack of cooperation, and, in general, resistance to change.

COLLABORATIVE STRUCTURE

Authority Paths and Decision Processes

An important evaluation process in a collaborative structure is peer evaluation, in which members of the group express how they feel about another group member's performance. However, this is not the only—or even the most important—evaluation process. Essentially, the most important evaluation process is that in which members of the organization as a whole express how they feel about a person's performance. In this case the manager seeks to collect information relative to the individual's performance and feed it back to the individual. As a rule, there is a fairly formal procedure associated with this: The individual is given feedback information sometimes by a panel of superiors and other times in a report by his or her manager that summarizes the responses of others toward the subordinate. Or the feedback may be in a combination of both forms. Often feedback is provided collectively and directly to the group in the form of control reports designating weak spots in the productivity of the group. This is then focused on a particular individual who is performing the task that creates the weak spot. This feedback is general knowledge to the total group, where each person knows how the other is doing. This system is informal and, except in extreme situations, tends to avoid direct confrontation between the manager and the group member. Instead, the group handles the situation by putting pressure on the individual involved.

Information Flow and Information Systems

In a collaborative structure, feedback on group performance and information on quality and quantity standards is directed to the group and shared by all the group's members. Such performance data is provided to help the group correct its own problems and tends to be an appraisal, and the group usually deals with it directly. An approach of this nature is problem-oriented, which focuses more on the task than on the individual and his or her contributing behavior.

Individual and Organizational Relationship

A collaborative structure encourages general peer evaluation. In such a structure there is likely to be a fairly high level of trust and support among group members—an attitude of "Watch out for your buddy and your buddy'll watch out for you." Provided the individual members of the organization are not at great variance with the norms and prescribed standards of the organization as a whole, all members will receive fair group evaluations. There tends to be a low level of excuse-making and relatively high level of ownership in the organization's tasks. How the total organization achieves its goals is usually of low concern to members of the group; collaborative structure fosters an attitude of "That's the company's problem, not mine."

COORDINATIVE STRUCTURE

Authority Paths and Decision Process

In a coordinative structure, as contrasted with a bureaucratic structure, individual workers evaluate their own results. They make judgments about how well they are performing against previously agreed targets and are able to take steps to correct mistakes or problems they may have. Usually, there are broad policies that cover the use of information flow rather than define specific evaluation processes. Such a policy may simply be a broad statement of management philosophy, such as: "We operate under the concept of Management by Objectives." In a coordinative structure, feedback flows directly to the individual —with duplicate information going to the manager and other organization members who need it in order to accomplish their tasks. It is expected that the individual will deal with his or her own deviations from agreed-to targets and will seek out the information and assistance necessary to achieve his or her goals.

Information Flow and Information Systems

In a coordinative system, information flows directly to the individual, who is then able to make a self-evaluation on the basis of how well he or she has achieved his or her goals. This type of information flow requires that the individual be given complete and accurate information immediately following the performance of his or her work. In a production situation, for example, a person completing the building of a particular unit would check the unit to see if it meets quality standards. A manager would be evaluating himself or herself against a set of predetermined targets (goals), looking for the areas in which his or her performance was less that had been agreed on. Such targets would be broader than those of the individual worker and would involve the contributing results of many people working for him or her.

Here we have a formalized system of goals and definitions as a part of a goal-setting process. Appraisal would be formal; however, evaluation processes would focus on task accomplishment rather than on personality. It would work something like this: At the beginning of a work assignment or work period an individual would sit down with his or her superior and identify the task to be accomplished, specifying the targets or standards toward which he or she would be working, defining the plan of action, and designating the checkpoints along the way. At these checkpoints the individual would be making evaluations of his or her own performance, establishing procedures for dealing with deviations in results, and enlisting the assistance and help of other individuals, including his or her superior, when such assistance is needed. Because of his or her sense of responsibility toward others in the organization, each individual will seek information relevant to the job at hand from all sources, not just from within his or her own group. The focus *would not* be on personality, but rather on task problem-solving directed at goal achievement.

Individual and Organizational Relationships

Since self-evaluation (as opposed to evaluation by peers or superiors) is primarily the responsibility of the individual, there tends to be little conflict between how individuals see themselves in the organization and how their bosses see them. The reason for this lower level of conflict is that the standards or targets against which each person is being measured are clear for all to see. Here people are aware that others know how they are doing against their predetermined goals. Therefore, each individual makes every attempt to keep his or her performance level above criticism by other members of the organization. The important point in this situation is that criticism comes from within the individual rather than from someone else. This type of evaluation relationship fosters a high level of trust, primarily due to the fact that information about a person's performance is so readily available. This puts accountability squarely on the shoulders of the individual and eliminates the excuses so common in a bureaucratic situation. It fosters high ownership on the part of the individual and develops his or her competency in planning and achieving objectives. The evaluation process in a coordinative structure is conducted by the individual who seeks information relative to his or her position within the organization specifically in terms of the job which he or she is planning and achieving objectives. The evaluation process in a coordinative structure is conducted by the individual who seeks information relative to his or her position within the organization specifically in terms of the job which he or she is attempting to accomplish.

In Chapters 5 through 8 we have discussed the *contributing job-related processes,* including staffing, goal-setting, work performance, and performance evaluation, as they contribute to development of managers. So far we have intentionally avoided giving you an integrated picture of exactly how these factors contribute to the developmental process. It should be fairly clear by now that the coordinative structure fosters a higher degree of commitment to individual managerial development than the bureaucratic and collaborative structures. We recognize, of course, that it is not possible in all cases to have a coordinative structure, and it then becomes necessary for you to seek out those aspects of your organization which can maximize manager development. If, as we propose, managers do in fact develop faster in a coordinative environment, we believe you should strive to include as many of the coordinative variables in job-related processes as possible.

In Chapter 9 we will attempt a more comprehensive integration of the information which we have provided in Chapters 5 through 8.

ANALYZING YOUR OWN ORGANIZATION

As we have done in the three preceding chapters, we would like you now to examine your own organization in terms of the performance evaluation processes. Use the work sheets which are provided to do this. We again suggest that you read the example prior to starting on your own organization.

Management development evaluation form
Performance evaluation: authority paths and decision processes

In each of the following sections pick the descriptive statement that most nearly describes your own organization. Make notations of differences.

Organizational practices	Circle one	Notation of where your organization differs
Section I 1. Superior evaluates individual. 2. Peer evaluation/total group evaluation. 3. Individuals evaluate self against goals.	① 2 3	We have an evaluation system where the boss calls the subordinate in once a year and tells him (or her) how he's doing — "take it or leave it" attitude.
Section II 1. No formal procedure to formal evaluation, forms, procedures, etc. 2. Formal group, peer, and individual evaluation (all, combination, or one) 3. Broad general policy. Not formal (MBO type).	① 2 3	We have formal policies, forms, and evaluations, and summaries are filed in Personnel.

Organizational practices	Circle one	Notation of where your organization differs
Section III 1. Feedback to manager. 2. Feedback to group. 3. Feedback to individual.	① 2 3	The boss gets data on my work and tells me about it.
Section IV		
Section V		

Management development evaluation form
Performance evaluation: information flow and information systems

In each of the following sections pick the descriptive statement that most nearly describes your own organization. Make notations of differences.

Organizational practices	Circle one	Notation of where your organization differs
Section I		
1. Indirect feedback on results (i.e., reports to top person who controls work of others).	①	*Reports to the top, then down to me; some exceptions but relatively few.*
2. Direct feedback to groups on unit results.	2	
3. Self-evaluation based on goal achievement.	3	
Section II		
1. Personality-oriented appraisal —to individual.	1	*There is a section for evaluating weaknesses and strengths; also personal goals are set up.*
2. Group- and job-oriented appraisal with some personality measures (standards of performance).	②	
3. Results measured against preset goals (not personality).	3	

Organizational practices	Circle one	Notation of where your organization differs
Section III 1. May or may not be formalized (i.e., forms procedures). 2. Usually formalized. 3. Formalized system of goal definition, no formal appraisal system.	① 2 3	Highly formalised, performance evaluation data is plugged into the individual's computerised record.
Section IV		
Section V		

Management development evaluation form
Performance evaluation: individual and organizational relationships

In each of the following sections pick the descriptive statement that most nearly describes your own organization. Make notations of differences.

Organizational practices	Circle one	Notation of where your organization differs
Section I		
1. Manager's evaluation seldom agrees with subordinates' evaluation. Subordinates must accept manager's evaluation.	①	If a person disagrees with his boss, he keeps it to himself.
2. Peer evaluation (in group) generally agrees with individual evaluation.	2	
3. No conflict in evaluation because individual evaluates self against preset goals.	3	
Section II		
1. Distrust and low level of loyalty.	①	Considerable distrust between boss and subordinate.
2. Fairly high trust level and loyalty in group.	2	
3. High level of trust.	3	

Organizational practices	Circle one	Notation of where your organization differs
Section III		If a person can't get work up to the boss's expectations, he or she usually blames it on the boss or someone else.
1. Excuses, blaming, and low ownership are typical behaviors.	①	
2. Excuses, blaming, and low ownership in work performed by outside groups.	2	
3. Low level of excuses, blaming, and shifting of ownership to others.	3	
Section IV		
Section V		

Management development evaluation summary and scores

Add up the numbers you have circled on each of the preceding sheets. Enter the totals in the space provided below, then add them up to get the overall total.

Authority paths and decision processes   _3_

Information flow and information systems   _4_

Individual and organizational relationships   _3_

                             Total   _10_

Next, record the total on the following scale. This will give you an indication of where your organization stands on this process in relation to the bureaucratic, collaborative, and coordinative organizations.

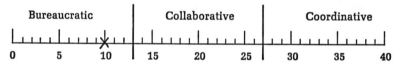

Bureaucratic   Collaborative   Coordinative

0   5   10   15   20   25   30   35   40

Observations and comments:

Now make your own evaluation on the pages that follow.

Management development evaluation form
Performance evaluation: authority paths and decision processes

---

In each of the following sections pick the descriptive statement that most nearly describes your own organization. Make notations of differences.

Organizational practices	Circle one	Notation of where your organization differs
Section I		
1. Superior evaluates individual.	1	
2. Peer evaluation/total group evaluation.	2	
3. Individuals evaluate self against goals.	3	
Section II		
1. No formal procedure to formal evaluation, forms, procedures, etc.	1	
2. Formal group, peer, and individual evaluation (all, combination, or one)	2	
3. Broad general policy. Not formal (MBO type).	3	

Organizational practices	Circle one	Notation of where your organization differs
Section III		
1. Feedback to manager.	1	
2. Feedback to group.	2	
3. Feedback to individual.	3	
Section IV		
Section V		

Management development evaluation form
Performance evaluation: information flow and information systems

In each of the following sections pick the descriptive statement that most nearly describes your own organization. Make notations of differences.

Organizational practices	Circle one	Notation of where your organization differs
Section I		
1. Indirect feedback on results (i.e., reports to top person who controls work of others.	1	
2. Direct feedback to groups on unit results.	2	
3. Self-evaluation based on goal achievement.	3	
Section II		
1. Personality-oriented appraisal —to individual.	1	
2. Group- and job-oriented appraisal with some personality measures (standards of performance).	2	
3. Results measured against preset goals (not personality).	3	

Organizational practices	Circle one	Notation of where your organization differs
Section III		
1. May or may not be formalized (i.e., forms procedures).	1	
2. Usually formalized.	2	
3. Formalized system of goal definition, no formal appraisal system.	3	
Section IV		
Section V		

Management development evaluation form
Performance evaluation: individual and organizational relationships

In each of the following sections pick the descriptive statement that most nearly describes your own organization. Make notations of differences.

Organizational practices	Circle one	Notation of where your organization differs
Section I		
1. Manager's evaluation seldom agrees with subordinates' evaluation. Subordinates must accept manager's evaluation.	1	
2. Peer evaluation (in group) generally agrees with individual evaluation.	2	
3. No conflict in evaluation because individual evaluates self against preset goals.	3	
Section II		
1. Distrust and low level of loyalty.	1	
2. Fairly high trust level and loyalty in group.	2	
3. High level of trust.	3	

Organizational practices	Circle one	Notation of where your organization differs
Section III		
1. Excuses, blaming, and low ownership are typical behaviors.	1	
2. Excuses, blaming, and low ownership in work performed by outside groups.	2	
3. Low level of excuses, blaming, and shifting of ownership to others.	3	
Section IV		
Section V		

Management development evaluation summary and scores

Add up the numbers you have circled on each of the preceding sheets. Enter the totals in the space provided below, then add them up to get the overall total.

Authority paths and decision processes   _____

Information flow and information systems   _____

Individual and organizational relationships   _____

                                     Total   _____

Next, record the total on the following scale. This will give you an indication of where your organization stands on this process in relation to the bureaucratic, collaborative, and coordinative organizations.

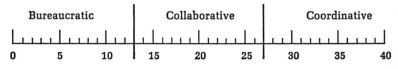

| Bureaucratic | Collaborative | Coordinative |

```
|_____|_____|_____|_____|_____|_____|_____|_____|
0     5    10    15    20    25    30    35    40
```

Observations and comments:

9/Integrating Factors Affecting MD

Increasing evidence supports the fact that a large number of recent college graduates, oftentimes only a year or two out of college, depart their organizations voluntarily either to go to other organizations or to go back to school. A possible explanation for this high turnover is the failure of many organizations to recognize what college graduates really want and what their values are relative to the work they are performing and to their lives in general; that is, that the organizational demands on the individual are often incongruous with his or her own sense of values, preferences, perceptions, interests, and desires.

ORGANIZATIONAL CONSTRAINTS

Observation and, to some extent, personal experience suggests that a person's own sense of what he or she would like to do with his or her own career is often subordinated to the requirements and needs of an organization. When individuals experience inconsistency between what they would like to do and what they think an organization expects them to do, they may cope with it by a number of alternative approaches. First, they may deny to themselves that there is any inconsistency. Second, they may rationalize their position and accept it. Third, they may strive to change their behavior so that it will become more consistent with the organizational requirements. And fourth, they may attempt to change the organizational practices and systems to be more consistent with their own interests and needs. And finally, they may recognize that the problem does exist but feel helpless to change it—and therefore withdraw from any active attempt to do so.

Frequently there are high degrees of incongruity between the needs of healthy people and the demands of their organization. The resulting effect of this is disturbance, in terms of frustration, failure, conflict within the individual and between the individual and the organization, and, in general, personal ineffectiveness. Usually, the adaptive behavior of the average person is to attempt to maintain some form of self-integration—and this can impede the ability of the individual to integrate himself or herself into the formal organizational structure. Thus incongruity between personal and organizational needs is a disadvantage to both the individual and the organization, since it means lost productivity, lost effectiveness, and lost time in terms of the individual's growth and development.

You will recall that in Chapter 4 we made reference to the question of the relationship between the individual's life style and the organization's basic characteristics. It is appropriate now to examine just what happens when the life style of an individual in an organization does not match these organizational structures and processes. Our purpose is (1) to emphasize the importance of understanding what the organizational structures consist of and (2) to determine whether those structures are suitable for maximizing the growth of the individual within the organization. Our contention throughout this book has been that the life style and values of the individual often are not consistent with the requirements of the organization, and we argue for compatibility between individual life style and organizational life style. To illustrate, a formalistic person would be best suited if employed by a bureaucratic organization; a personalistic individual would likely fit best into a coordinative structure.

We do not wish to lose sight of the fact that our basic belief is that organizations face the challenge of inventing and implementing structures which will permit various types of leaders to rise wherever relevant expert knowledge is located. Our assumption is that expertise does exist within each organization, and that to maximize the talents of its employees the organization should be so structured that the expertise can emerge. Basically we believe that the leadership skill, whatever that may mean, can be found anywhere within the organization and that a form of hierarchical structure will usually inhibit the leadership competency from developing. As we conceive of it, leadership in organizations of the future should be a series of functions that emerge from the nature of the people found in those organizations. The leadership role could be assumed by anybody within the organization—whatever that person's status, location, or position—just so long as he or she has knowledge and expertise to deal with the problem or issue at hand.

We recognize that this concept of leadership is somewhat at odds with the traditional notion; however, we base our conclusions on the simple fact that this is fundamentally the way humans naturally grow within their total environment.

CHANGING LIFE STYLES

An increasing amount of research supports the claim that dramatic changes are occurring in the life styles of our youth today. Yet, we should begin to look beyond the headlines and television broadcasts for the evidence and the repercussions of these changes. Looking simply at campus unrest, student rebellions, drug usage, draft-card burning, resistance to ROTC programs, general militancy on the part of young people, and so forth, is not sufficient to explain the change. There is growing evidence that the values and perspectives underlying these behaviors are durable, i.e., that they are here to be dealt with today and will not be gone tomorrow. They are not to be dismissed as a result of a temporary erratic phase which all youth go through.

Since in our definition life styles incorporate basic values and perspectives, they emerge very slowly and exist concurrently with more traditional orientations within our culture. We would like to describe very briefly three orientations, or basic value categories, that seem to prevail to varying degrees through our society today. They were identified and discussed in a Ph.D. dissertation prepared by Dr. Thomas E. Bier (Case Western Reserve University, 1967), who labeled them "formalistic," "sociocentric," and "personalistic."

Formalistic Orientation

The formalistic orientation stems from the industrial revolution and the ensuing era of highly structured bureaucracy. Formalistic individuals need to receive direction from authorities before they act. In most instances their behavior depends on what is acceptable to the organization. In a strict sense, they do what they are told; in a broader sense they work within boundaries or guidelines or in directions established by superiors, teachers, superordinate powers, or authorities.

Sociocentric Orientation

This is a social orientation which has evolved over the past 30 years concurrently with an increased emphasis on industrial humanism (human relations) and a consideration of the human or social aspects of organizations. The reactions of sociocentric individuals are preceded by discussion and agreement with others, in order to make sure that there is consensus in all cases. For sociocentrically oriented individuals the norms of the group are apt to be determined by each individual's behavior in relationship to interpersonal commitments, relationships, and group cohesion. Sociocentric individuals need to participate in important decisions that will affect them. Authority and hierarchy structures are minimized, and other individuals are viewed as peers or as colleagues. Individualism is valued and stressed. It is important for sociocentric individuals to act on their own, free of authority and direction, but they collectively establish with others the limits, goals, and standards by which they will control and direct themselves.

It's quite apparent that the sociocentric orientation among people has been increasing rapidly during the past several years. It's not hard to conceive that this may be a predominant orientation within a very few years to come.

Personalistic Orientation

This orientation has emerged most noticeably during the last 10 to 15 years, and is most apparent among college youth. Personalistic individuals look within themselves, consulting their own experiences for a sense of direction and purpose.

The behavioral characteristics of each of these three orientations are described in greater detail in Fig. 9.1. The arrows moving from left to right in the upper part of the figure indicate that an increasing proportion of people in our society tends to be more sociocentric and personalistic. Conversely, a decreasing portion of our population holds formalistic orientation. As you now can see, the behavioral factors of the three orientations differ markedly.

The beliefs of personalistic individuals are largely determined by their current experiences, and their involvement with and

Fig. 9.1 The present trend in change of social orientation, from formalistic to personalistic

Behavioral factors	Formalistic ⟶	Sociocentric ⟶	⟶ Personalistic
Basis of action	Direction from authorities	Discussion, agreement with others	Direction from within
Form of control	Rules, laws, policies	Interpersonal commitments	What I think is right or needed
Responsibility to	Superordinate powers	Peers, colleagues, self	Self
Desired end	Compliance	Consensus, agreement	Actualization of individual
To be avoided	Deviation from authoritative direction	Failure to reach agreement	Not being oneself
To get material goods	Compete	Collaborate	Take for granted
Basis for growth	Following the established order	Interaction	Acting on awareness of self
Position relative to others	Member of hierarchy	Peer-group member	Separate individual
Identify with/loyal to	Organization	Group	Individual
Time perspective	Future	Near future	Present

questioning of those experiences and their environment. Their feeling is that experience must be concrete, vivid, personal, "now." Personally oriented individuals are tuned to the present rather than to the future, and the present must provide them with meaningful involvement. They seek meaningfulness in individuality, and the actualization of their own potential and uniqueness toward greater excitement, satisfaction, and fulfillment.

If personalistic individuals do not experience personal involvement or meaning, they have no basis for commitment—and therefore feel less honor bound to fulfill commitments. This makes them less dependable workers than individuals with other orientations. Their commitments and loyalties are not to organizations or groups, nor to positions, status, or authority, but to their own experience and feelings, and they strongly resist what they consider attempts by others to deny the validity of their world. Personalistic individuals criticize traditional beliefs of what constitutes a successful life (though of course they are not the only ones to do so), organizations and institutions which they view as blocking their desires to live meaningful and unique lives, social norms and beliefs that they consider destructive to those desires, and behavior and expression by others which they judge to be inconsistent with personalistic values and beliefs. Just as personalistically oriented individuals view themselves as unique, so they view other people, and they expect that others should be treated the same as they would like to be treated.

Such individuals value a community of noncompetitive, nonexploitive relationships in which the ethic of social service replaces the ethic of hard work, and while they are rapidly increasing in number, it is not too surprising that they currently represent a minority of people in organizations.

ORGANIZATIONAL STRUCTURES AND LIFE STYLES

Up to this point in our discussion we have been dealing primarily with basic changes in the nature of the people in our society. It is now appropriate to look at the changes taking place in organizations to emphasize how mismatches occur between organization structure and processes and the individuals within organizations.

As we previously said, more and more individuals are developing a sociocentric orientation in which actions and values are based on participation, collaboration, integration, and consensus from group interaction and discussion. We even see in the near future the need for organizations to respond to the personalistic individual, who we believe sees, as we have previously mentioned, a more natural way for individuals to live and grow within an organization. Conversely, it is not hard to see that responsiveness to external authority rules, policy, laws, material rewards, or organization demands will decrease in the future. That is to say, the more formalistic type of organizational structure will be changed to be responsive to the types of individuals living within our organization. By our definition, the connecting link between the people required to live in our organizations and the jobs that they will perform is the organizational structure itself. When that structure is inconsistent with orientation of the people within the organization, the result is incongruity, which brings about decreased effectiveness and productivity, and increased frustration, anxiety, and alienation. We see a movement of organizational structures and processes from the bureaucratic structure to what we earlier referred to as an organic structure. Figure 9.2, which was prepared by Dr. Frank Friedlander (Case Western Reserve University), shows the differences between the bureaucratic structure and the emerging organizational structures along the lines previously discussed.

There are several basic questions that we would like to raise at this point. First, how well will the bureaucratic type structure, which exists in most of our organizations today, fit the needs of socially and personally oriented individuals, particularly in terms of their own development growth? To what extent will these structures point to and facilitate human growth and development for the individual? What must organizations do in order to foster and encourage the optimization of the individual's own natural growth processes?

It is our conviction and belief that as the sociocentric and personalistic orientations emerge, the ability of the bureaucratic

Fig. 9.2 The present trend in change of organizational structure, from bureaucratic to organic

Organization function	Bureaucratic structure	→ Organic structure
Activities	Narrow, single purpose categories of activities; coordination at higher levels of hierarchy	Overlapping, integrative, interdependent, shared activities
Authority	Authority vested in higher level in hierarchy	Authority vested in expertise; developed through mutual influence
Communication	Direct communication along hierarchical lines; defined mechanisms; instructive and directive; coordination via mechanical means	Infusing and diffusing in many directions; searching process for sources of information; advisory and consultative; coordination via people
Decision-making	Decisions along hierarchical lines; hierarchically imposed decisions	Decisions via mutual influence; evolving and interpretative decision process in broad decision structure
Objectives	Precise and clear; objectives are determined and imposed by hierarchy	Interpretive; local objective important; objectives established by mutual influence objectives are part of shared beliefs and values
Role expectations	Well-defined prior to task definition Defined by authority Stable Specified	Ill-defined prior to task definition Defined with colleagues Flexible Seeking out
Relationships	One-to-one relations Long-term relationships Groups with stable membership Familiar members Conflict suppressed Expertise defined by hierarchical role Hierarchical coordination Dependence upon hierarchy	Links with many Temporary relationships Groups with changing membership Strangers Conflict utilized Expertise sought out in organization Collaboration Interdependence with colleagues

structure to maximize human growth in individuals will decrease. Thus, the more bureaucratic the organizational structure, the more it will repel the socially and personally oriented individual. On the other hand, the more organic the structure, the more likely it will be to satisfy the needs and basic growth drives of the personalistic and sociocentric individual. In other words, organizations need to become more participative and collaborative, allowing individuals to integrate and to be consulted on decisions that affect their growth and development.

Very many people doubt whether organizations can, in fact, adapt to the personal orientation. Organic structures demand interdependence rather than independence; collaboration and integration must evolve from the task group rather than from within each individual; groups must work as teams rather than having each individual do his own thing. This raises the question of whether organizations *can* be designed in such a way that the individual can be independent while at the same time functioning as a part of an organization.

We realize that there are no simple answers to the questions we have raised; we do not have a cookbook with immediate answers that we can offer organizations. One thing does seem clear, however: we must find ways in which to design organizational structures and processes to maximize the naturally human growth drives which are prevalent, it is estimated, in over 50 percent of our work force today. If we plan to effectively develop future managers, we cannot avoid the questions we have raised here.

An Example

Perhaps an example would help to make our point. Suppose a young man comes to work for us who tends to be sociocentric with some tendency toward a personalistic orientation. He is concerned with direction from within himself as well as with reaching agreement on issues involving other people. He looks to himself for the primary sources of responsibility but is concerned about how other people feel within the organization and within his group. He is highly actualizing in his orientation and is interested in developing his skills, but he is also interested in helping other people develop theirs. He believes that one should be oneself and not a phony, but also that it is necessary to reach agreement on various points. He is oriented to the present and not concerned too much about next year at this time. His main thrust in life seems to be to develop his own skills without hampering or hindering others from doing the same. He is highly intelligent and action-oriented.

This young man is employed by a large corporation which has put him into a training program. Let us assume that this corporation is by definition a bureaucratic structure: Its activities are narrow in scope; authority is vested in higher levels of the hierarchy; direct communication flows from the top down through the organization, but not in other directions; decisions are along hierarchical lines; objectives are clear and concise; role expectations are well-defined in terms of job descriptions; relationships are on a one-to-one basis (boss to subordinate); status is very important; and the organization is highly dependent on its "rule book" to get the job done.

Our hypothetical individual comes into the organization expecting to develop, grow and expand his own sense of awareness as well as helping others to do the same. He immediately, on entry into the company, is slotted into a specific job. He is told to follow the basic rules and practices of the firm, and when decisions are to be made he should check immediately with the boss. He is also given very clear and precise data relative to the task which he is supposed to accomplish and the relationship and arrangements with others in the organization.

It is not hard to see how this particular individual will come into conflict with the organization. In terms which we have previously used, there will be an inconsistency between his own values and beliefs and the way in which the organization functions. The odds are that this individual will drop out of the organization rather early, or that he may become an irritant to the organization through his efforts to try to change it. It is quite unlikely that he will develop his skills to any great extent within this environment.

The point is that had this individual gone into a more organic type structure, the odds are that he would have found a far more compatible environment and in turn would have developed his leadership abilities and potential within the firm.

CONCLUSION

Our purpose in this chapter, as you will recall, is to help you integrate the basic information you have collected about your own organization with an understanding of the life style of the individuals within your organization. From this you should be able to make some prediction about how successful you will be in developing potential managers. Where inconsistency exists between the individual and the organization, it is predictable that human growth and development will be minimal. Where the sociocentric orientaticn matches the organic structure, it is predictable that human growth and development will be at a high level. There is some reasonable question about whether personalistic individuals would be able to function effectively and grow and develop on their own terms within organic structures; however, they would find them far more compatible than formalistic structures. We believe that formalistic individuals in bureaucratic structures will be able to function effectively, but with a minimum amount of human growth and development. They will appear within the organization to be following career paths and growth toward higher leadership roles, but it is unlikely that the unique or creative aspects of their make-up will be developed. It is also unlikely that they would find themselves successful in any organizations other than the bureaucratic.

In the next chapter we will complete the integration by showing how all of this works for you. Again we would like to stress that we do not have all the answers; at this point we are working with concepts which we believe are predictive of the Management Development Processes for the future.

10/Problems in Designing MD Processes

In the preceding chapters we examined the major structures or processes of organizations, the principal life styles of individuals in organizations, and the relationships that exist between those two subjects.

In Chapters 1 and 2 we laid out a conceptional framework which served as a basis for the remaining chapters. We contended that there are three different types of structures and processes within organizations: bureaucratic, collaborative, and coordinative. We argued that three critical factors directly contribute to how managers develop: authority paths and decision processes, information flow and information systems, and the way in which individuals relate to one another within an organization. We also argued that staffing, goal-setting, the performance of work, and the evaluation process are critical mediating factors which tend to impede or speed up the developmental process. Our contention has been that when an individual with a given type of life style is part of an organization with an appropriate basic character, the mediating organizational factors lead to congruency with that individual, which, in turn, will maximize his or her management growth and development. Our underlying assumption is that the natural learning process (i.e., the way in which most people learn throughout their lives) is the only functional way for people to grow and develop within an organization. We argue finally that many of our organizations have, in fact, done little or nothing to stimulate natural growth in people.

The basic concept is fairly easy to grasp, but making it operational is another question. This chapter addresses that question directly, explaining how you may take the ideas which we have discussed and plug them into your organization.

We have asked you to participate in the learning process by completing the survey sheets at the end of Chapters 5, 6, 7, and 8. At the conclusion of this chapter we will summarize how you may use the data you have accumulated to alter your organization to accommodate the basic human needs of the people in it. Before doing so, however, we believe that it would be worthwhile to go over some of the complications which managers frequently encounter in making MD work, to discuss how we believe a manager should approach the problem of developing managers, and to explain some of the blocks to an understanding of the Organizational Development approach to Management Development.

PROBLEMS WITHIN MD

When managers are confronted with a question of what they are doing to enhance the development of their staff, they usually acknowledge that they do have some responsibility, perhaps referring to some directive or policies issued to them by a higher level of authority. But inwardly they deny that they have any responsibility for the development of management. The problem is that managers do not recognize the effect that they personally have on the individuals whom they have working for them. Before a manager can encourage management development in others, he must recognize the responsibility which he carries in this regard.

Another difficulty is that managers frequently see management development as programmatic, something somebody else can do for them. They see it, in other words, as simply sending someone off to a seminar course in some distant city. They do not recognize that real development takes place within the context of their relationship with their subordinates.

But even when managers recognize that management development is one of their major responsibilities, even when they see that it relates to the work itself, as well as other mediating variables, they often find it difficult to understand just what is involved in a workable approach for their own organizations. To put it another way, they do not systematically develop their own human diagnostic skills in the same way that they do their financing, marketing, and other business skills. For managers to successfully use the concepts we have discussed in this book, they must understand and recognize the need for a systematic approach to the development of human resources.

In trying to understand how people grow and develop, managers often fail to recognize the need for congruency between the individual and the organization of which he or she is a part. It is important for managers to recognize that there must be a good fit between individuals and the organizational processes before those individuals will develop a high degree of task orientation and, in turn, receive the kind of human fulfillment and growth which they are seeking. This suggests that managers should have a fairly high degree of flexibility; that is, a willingness to adjust the nature of jobs and relationships in such a way that they maximize the individual's goal orientation.

Finally, most managers also have difficulty in developing other managers because they just don't know how people grow and develop their skills and competencies. Most of us have traditionally, through the educational processes, come to believe that the best way for people to grow and develop is through exposure to some sort of classroom format. We do not question the necessity for and value of this type of education; we suggest only that it has limitations, and that as people mature they learn more from practical experience and from what they teach themselves. (Consider, for example, that most institutions of higher learning require that the majority of their students do laboratory and field work, and that they serve internships for advanced degrees—all of which recognizes the role of experiencing through "natural learning processes.") In order to make the OD approach to MD work, a manager must first have a strong commitment to the basic notion that human beings *do* learn through their own experiences and *can* be self-teachers when the opportunity is provided. The whole thrust of this book has been to encourage you to view MD along this line.

APPROACHING THE MD PROCESS

We can make a number of specific suggestions to managers who are interested in improving their ability to diagnose conditions and redesign them for maximum human growth and development. Those suggestions are as follows:

1. Managers need to study and understand the ways in which individuals grow and develop. The idea of natural growth is not enough. You must try to see how each person working for you can be stimulated through his or her environment to strive toward self-actualization and the maximization of his or her own growth and development. There is no easy answer to this ques-

tion, of course, except to continually practice looking for the various conditions which "turn people on."

2. It is important that managers understand something about the variations in life styles of those people working for them. Such understanding can be achieved by a number of different approaches; e.g., by use of a life style questionnaire,* by the development of insights through conversations and interviews, and by creation of a personal inventory for each individual. When you have become familiar with the basic natures of the people working for you, you determine how well the organizational processes previously discussed apply to them. You may decide that the organizational processes are correct as they stand, and that the employees should fit the processes—or you may decide to alter your organization's processes to fit the employees. Either way, you achieve greater congruency for individuals.

3. You need to understand the organizational structure: how it inhibits communications, how it inhibits the flow of information, how people work together within it, how decisions are made within it. Failure to understand it can create serious problems for managers who think the system is functioning in one way when, in fact, it is functioning in quite a different way. One good way to acquire an understanding of the organizational structure would be to carefully analyze the actual flow of information, the relationships, and the decisions and approaches used to accomplish the job. Outside consultants can help you do this, but we believe that the most practical approach would be to use the resources which are available to you within your own organization—your own people.

4. Managers need to understand themselves. This involves knowing their leadership style and how it fits them, how they affect the people working for them, how they are perceived by those people, and how this inhibits or enhances human growth and development within the organization. There are several ways to achieve understanding in this area. Managers can: solicit information from the people working for them (which

---

* Dr. Frank Friedlander, Case Western Reserve University, Cleveland, Ohio, has developed such a questionnaire.

requires a high degree of trust); acquire information from other sources, such as a personal-growth T-group (training group); or simply become more introspective, examining their own reactions to various stimuli. We believe that all of these approaches are useful. The T-group, which increases self-awareness, makes it possible for a person to be more introspective and creative, and to achieve a higher degree of trust from others in the organization. Increased trust makes it possible for people to give a manager more feedback.

5. Managers need to be able to match human resources (people) to organizational processes. They must develop analytical skills to help them understand how the various factors affect one another.

6. Managers should be able to bring about changes within the organizational processes which unpredictably enhance and stimulate management development and they need to develop their skills in designing such approaches. Not only should they have good design skills, but they must also be able to test the approaches being used and measure the results.

7. Finally, managers must avoid becoming locked into one way of doing things. They must be flexible about the approaches they use, allowing themselves to be influenced both by the system and by its human members. If managers can do good design work, are willing to test and evaluate their own results, and are flexible, it is quite probable that they will be able to come up with systems which will maximize the MD processes within their organizations.

BLOCKS TO MD

By way of summary, there are a number of basic factors that tend to block managers from being able to evaluate their own organizations and bring about the changes which are necessary for human growth and development to be maximized. The first of these is the managers' own style of management. Authoritarian type managers probably will not be able to take advantage of the natural human growth and development process, whereas participatory or get-involved type managers are likely to do so.

Secondly, many managers are not willing to invest the time required to bring about the changes that maximize growth and development. They often see such activity as a subsidiary job, or an "add-on" responsibility, hence something to do in the evening or possibly on Saturdays, but not on a day-to-day basis. However, anyone wishing to become fully engaged in helping people grow and develop must be willing to invest the time. We estimate that the manager should spend about 50 percent of his or her time on this process.

Finally, managers' own values and beliefs may be one of the major blocks to their ability to use the approach prescribed in this book. To illustrate: After reading this far, you yourself may have concluded that this is all well and good, but not for you. If you examine why you have reached this conclusion, you will probably find that it is because of some basic values you hold about how organizations ought to function. You might say to yourself, for example, "It really doesn't make any difference how the individual feels about it, it is what I want that really counts, so that's what we're going to have around here." This attitude leads to the conditions found in a bureaucratic structure, in which people change only because of the personal threat which exists within such organizations. It does not encourage the natural human growth and development processes.

Managers need to examine their own beliefs about how their organizations function. If they see their organizations as bureaucratic, then they should carefully examine the nature of the people working in such structures, as well as how they expect or anticipate those people will develop. As we previously mentioned, bureaucratic managers with formalistic people can only expect their people to do precisely as they are told. And it would be unreasonable to expect those people to develop their own plans when they have plans already laid out for them.

IN REVIEW OF THE BASIC MD MODEL

Although it may seem somewhat redundant to restate our basic approach to management development, we believe that it would be worthwhile at this time. The model was originally presented in Chapter 2.

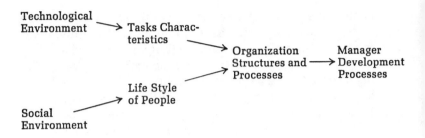

You will recall that we discussed how organizational processes and structures must be matched to tasks and life styles. We argued that: (1) technological aspects affect tasks, (2) social aspects affect life styles, (3) both are generally given in most organizations. When tasks, life styles, and organizational processes are congruent, we maximize the MD processes. We devoted most of our time to an examination of the organizational processes in three types of structures: bureaucratic, collaborative, and coordinative.

In the preceding chapters we set forth a basic procedure by which you could examine your organization. Within this format, you were encouraged to describe your organization as you see it. Just as in the illustration we presented, you probably found that your own organizational processes ranged perhaps from a bureaucratic to a coordinative approach. Rarely is an organizational structure entirely of one type; it is usually a mixure of all three. This adds to the complexity of the problem of analyzing and designing the best approach to be used within your organization.

In our model we have not dealt directly with the nature of the human resources already available in your organization. We have assumed here that you will be able to analyze and summarize that nature as it exists now, on the basis of our discussions, so we leave it to you to examine the human resources and match them with the appropriate organizational processes.

Finally, consult Fig. 10.1. By applying the example shown there, together with the information presented earlier in this book, it will be possible for you to reshape your organization in such a way that it maximizes the management development process.

Fig. 10.1 Analysis of organizational processes and human factors (example)

1. Organizational process scores
(See ends of Chapters 5, 6, 7, 8)

	Score	Type Structure
Staffing Practices	24	Collaborative (High)
Goal-Setting Processes	15	Collaborative (Low)
Work Performance	15	Collaborative (Low)
Evaluation Processes	10	Bureaucratic (High)

$$\text{Total} \div 4 \qquad \frac{64}{4} = 16 = \text{Collaborative (Low)}$$

2. Life style of organizational members

Number of Members 11

Life Style by Individual (estimated) (see Fig. 9.1)

Person	Estimate	Person	Estimate	Life Style Totals
A	F	G	F	F = 2
B	S	H	S	S = 7
C	S	I	S	P = 2
D	S	J	P	
E	P	K	S	
F	S			

Specific organization process changes
(Refer to worksheets at ends of Chapters 5, 6, 7, 8)

First emphasis should be placed on changing the evaluation processes, including development of:

1. More peer evaluation and group developmental assistance
2. More information about performance going to smaller units in the organization
3. More specific and formalized evaluation processes
4. Higher trust level between management and members of the organization
5. Strengthening of loyalty to individual's immediate work group

Comments and analysis →

Organizational members are predominantly sociocentric. The two formalistic members are older men past the age where they are eligible for major advancement in the organization.

The two personalistic members bear watching and special tailoring of their developmental plans, since the organizational processes will be most congruent with the sociocentric members of the organization.

11/Measures of a Successful MD/OD Approach

We have emphasized the importance of the manager's actively thinking about his or her own organization and the MD environment which hinders or helps individual development. We have also assumed that you have been completing the worksheets at the end of those chapters in which they appear. From these things you should have a fairly clear picture of the practices you are using and their effect on the people working for you. You probably have reached some general conclusions relative to the strengths and weaknesses of your approach. You may be wondering, "How will I know whether the approach I am using will actually facilitate management development?" What we need now is a reasonably accurate way of measuring the results of your MD effort.

Management development, as you must recognize, lacks specific and predictable technological theories; it is, in fact, basically a fine art, much as are the fields of medicine, drama, and music. Since MD is a fine art, the only way you can be sure that your practices are working is to keep trying new techniques and approaches and measuring the results. It appears, therefore, that the development of managers involves trial and error; that we must try and practice varying approaches until we learn which one works best for us. This suggests that you must, at the very least, become more aware of what is going on in your organization, and how your manager development practices affect the organization, directly or indirectly.

THE NATURE OF CHANGES

The changes you will be instituting will fall into three categories, involving:

1. Organizational practices, policies, procedures, forms, and techniques which are used to get the work accomplished.

2. Your own leadership style, as well as the leadership practices of those people working for you. This has to do with the way in which you relate to the people in your organization, and the effect that boss/subordinate relationships have on productivity, interest, desire, and sense of personal achievement.

3. The overall philosophy that underlies your actions. For example, I may believe that people perform better when they are told specifically what to do—and this directs how I relate to subordinates.

What is needed is the way to measure the effect of the changes. When we make changes, we need to be able to examine the resulting relationship between cause and effect. We must understand, though, that in measuring MD results, it is difficult to follow a direct relationship between a program or a change and the way a person develops. Usually change involves a multiple effect; that is, several interrelated things affect each other during the change process.

Evidence of Change

Within an organizational context, it is often obvious that change is taking place. It is also true that the causes of the change may not be the least bit obvious. For instance, such things as decreased turnover, decreased absenteeism, under-spending budgets, and the like may be readily identified as the desired results of a specific change—but just as often they may not.

When you examine the MD aspects of your responsibility in a more organic (i.e., collaborative) environment, you may find the following indications of an environment conducive to growth:

1. Individuals may:

a) Become more innovative; that is, they may create things, or come up with ideas and suggestions which they have not been doing in the past.

b) Tend to be more open. They may be willing to admit and own up to things they're doing and the feelings they have.

c) Be more willing to speak out on issues which, in fact, they have not spoken out on in the past.

d) Express feelings about the organization which are more positive than they have been in the past.

e) Express the desire for enriching types of experiences, asking for opportunities to participate in task forces, to be involved in committee activities, to attend seminars, etc.

f) Express feelings about themselves which are more positive; that is to say, their egos and self-esteem will tend to be higher.

g) Be able to express more clearly their career interests and approaches to reaching their career objectives and goals. They will have clear ideas about what they want to do and how they want to do it.

h) Tend to take more risks and accept responsibility for them. They will experiment with ways of doing things which they have not done in the past. They will blame other people less for their own mistakes.

2. The organization will:

a) Be more flexible and adaptive about meeting the emergencies and situations which arise. For example, an organization confronted with a major competitive change in the marketplace will be able to rally around that problem in a relatively short period of time and solve it.

b) Share leadership responsibility with individuals who feel able to move ahead in the organization. Individuals will take on responsibility for their portion of the job.

c) Encourage more cooperation between people in the organization. This doesn't mean that the conflict will necessarily be less; it simply means that people will find ways to work together more effectively.

d) Find that indicators of performance, such as profitability, productivity, etc., will tend to go up.

A growth-encouraging, challenging, and stimulating organization is one in which people accept the responsibility for their own actions and are willing to help others in accomplishing ing their objectives.

Within the bureaucratic structure you will find the following indicators of how MD is progressing:

1. Individuals will:

a) Tend to follow the rules and conform to the accepted patterns of doing things within the organization.

b) Tend to hold back their suggestions and ideas, presenting them only when asked.

c) Show a minimal amount of commitment toward the organization, tending to give the organization what it expects and no more. They frequently feel that learning is generally not encouraged except as it relates to the specific objectives and tasks of the organization.

d) Not seem "turned on." Although they are not generally withdrawn, it takes a major disaster such as a major drop in profits to get them to actively seek solutions and changes.

e) Frequently be unwilling to express their career goals, feeling that it is important to keep those goals to themselves and reveal them only at the right moment.

f) Take only the risks that are assigned to them, and accept responsibility only for the job that has been assigned.

2. The organization will:

a) Tend to be less flexible and slower to adapt to new conditions. This isn't to say that the organization does not change, only that change involves an appreciable time lag (which can itself sometimes create undesirable new conditions).

b) Find that its people generally are unwilling to assume unassigned responsibilities. Therefore, the top manager ends up with those responsibilities which people down in the organization are not willing to accept.

c) Tend to show a higher level of conflict than other types of organizations, usually in what might be called borderline areas—areas in which individuals' jobs tend to overlap, and where authority and responsibility are not clearly defined.

d) Generally find that operating results are moderate in comparison with potential results.

We hope it is obvious now that our point of view very much favors an environment that is collaborative and "growthful" (i.e., conducive to growth) over a more bureaucratic environment. This is not because we are opposed to the bureaucratic structure—we recognize that there are organizations in which this is perhaps the best or most desirable structure—but because we believe that even in highly bureaucratic situations a movement in the direction of a more growthful organic structure has merit.

Some Typical Measurement Indicators

The list of ways in which your MD effort can be monitored or measured is probably endless, but we have selected just a few of those ways to look at here.

1. *Results:* It is obvious that results are the first indication of a healthy, growthful environment. When you see people producing more and higher quality work, when you see them meeting and exceeding their schedules, when you see increased profitability in the organization, you are probably witnessing the results of an environment which is conducive to individual growth and development.

2. *Feeling About the Organization:* In a growthful organization you will see individuals expressing feelings about the organization in their conversations, which manifest their interest and excitement about the organization. There is likely to be a lower level of grumbling and complaining about the organization and some people may show their interest in the organization by staying overtime, working on projects not directly connected with their own work, and helping others solve problems.

3. *Expenditures and Times Devoted to Learning:* Where an organization is providing a growthful environment, you can expect that the requests for educational expenditures will increase. Also, more time will be requested for outside learning experiences. More management time will be devoted to helping individuals improve their performance, and inside MD activities and programs will require a higher budget.

One word of caution: You should not assume that just by spending more money you are creating an enriched environment for growth and development. The MD expenditures should be a result of the need for growthful opportunities and organization. These needs should come from people in the body of the organization, not from someone at the head.

4. *Flexibility.* The organization's ability to solve its problems and deal with those issues that confront it will be improved. Responsibility for determining approaches and reaching solutions will be shared, not left to one person. Flexibility and growth characteristics of an organization will be manifest in the way in which people react to a particular problem; in a growthful environment people will react in an organized and orderly way; in a traditional environment people will manifest alarm and concern.

5. *Innovation:* In an environment conducive to individual growth you will see people moving ahead with their own ideas and making suggestions without fear of threat or reprimand.

6. *The Number of People Moving Up in the Organization:* Another indicator of the success of MD is the mobility of personnel. Employees are promoted or transferred within an organization because they are in demand—they bring desirable qualities to their new position. And when individuals feel that they can influence their own moves within an organization, that's another sign that MD efforts are paying off, for it means that employees perceive the environment as allowing individuals to experiment with their own career development plans.

We realize that the six ways of measuring the results of your MD efforts are a bit undefined in terms of your specific problems. We would suggest that you take the various indicators that seem to fit your organization and set up ways of measuring within your organization.

Measurement Techniques

There are several approaches that can be used to collect information useful in evaluating the effectiveness of your MD change effort.

1. Your actual observation of the changes taking place in your organization is probably one of the most reliable and valid ways you can measure change. What you see and hear can tell you whether you are succeeding.

2. Sensing instruments can be used—such as questionnaires,

group discussion meetings, and simply the questions asked in interviews with employees and subordinates.

3. Various kinds of statistical and cost reports can be used —including budget, performance records, and achievement of objectives.

4. Other sources of information include feedback from sources outside the organization—such as customers, clients, and people with whom your staff members come in contact. Such information serves to help you sense how your potential managers are reacting to the changes you have made.

With the above thoughts we conclude this book. We hope some new ideas have been presented that can be useful to you. We ask you to remember that people develop and grow because they have experienced a need to grow and have planned their own development in an environment which encourages their efforts.

Appendix

Bureaucratic organizational structure: relationship of mediating variables to MD

(I) Job-related processes contributing to MD	(II) Mediating organizational variables		
	Authority paths and decision processes	Information flow and information systems	Individual and organizational relationships
Staffing processes (Job placement)	1. Manager alone recommends individual for promotion. 2. Top manager makes choice. Individual has little influence. 3. Promotion within functional speciality. 4. Simple policies and procedures.	1. Manager "scouts out" candidates within and outside his organization. 2. Individual unaware of openings throughout organization. 3. No record system for identification of individuals. 4. Individual aware of unit openings by observation.	1. Individual's disagreement with organization job plan not considered. Limited cooperation. 2. Most competitive (political person) wins job. 3. Low trust in selection decision. 4. Most local person most likely to succeed. 5. Job placement counseling of personnel.
Goal-setting processes (Defining expected results)	1. Quotas/production standards. 2. Set by third party (ind. Engr-Time Study). 3. Serial goals: i.e., each person has segment of larger goal. 4. Inflexible.	1. Goals set at top and processed to lower levels through organizational channels. 2. Little upward feedback on goal validity. 3. Little or no formal systems and procedure.	1. Individuals' goals often in conflict with organization goals. 2. Limited individual cooperation and commitment toward assigned goals. 3. Individual does not see interdependency of own goals with others. 4. No help in setting goals.
Work performance (How work is done)	1. Specific step-by-step "how to" job description (narrow functions). 2. Changes made by higher authority. 3. Serial flow of work.	1. Only work-related information needed for individual to get the job done is provided. 2. Individual does not offer constructive suggestions. 3. Well developed central control systems.	1. Conflict between persons suppressed, negotiated by third party. 2. Cooperation limited to emergencies. 3. Individuals don't feel responsibility to others.
Evaluation processes (How work results are evaluated)	1. Superior evaluates individual. 2. No formal procedure to formal evaluation forms, procedures, etc. 3. Feedback to manager.	1. Indirect feedback on results (i.e., reports to top person who controls work of others. 2. Personality oriented appraisal—to individual. 3. May or may not be formalized (i.e., use forms and procedures).	1. Manager evaluation seldom agrees with subordinate's evaluation. Subordinates must accept manager's evaluation. 2. Distrust, low level of loyalty. 3. Excuses, blaming, and low ownership are typical behaviors.
MD practices Programs, systems, procedures suitable to I and II above	1. Managers decide who gets trained (usually individual). 2. Formal (off work) in-company and outside programs used. 3. From no formal policies to highly formalized. 4. Individual has little influence over decisions.	1. Management information shared with individual if manager desires. 2. No system for information dissemination. 3. MD programs carefully designed to control information made available. 4. Officials speak to organization via house organ, MD programs, etc.	1. How to discipline is taught managers. 2. How to direct and control are top priority subjects in MD. 3. Theory and leadership taught. 4. Well defined relationship spelled out in policies and procedures.
Behavior outputs Behavior to be expected from individual	1. Respond in predicted way. 2. Follow rules, norms. 3. Retain learning, apply later. 4. Not adaptive to radical changes.	1. Not offer constructive ideas and suggestions. 2. Search for information through informed sources. 3. Distort information.	1. Managers crack down on disagreement. 2. Managers exercise power of position to get results. 3. Not help solve organization problems. 4. Withdraw or leave organization if good opportunity comes along (low mobility).

Collaborative organizational structure: relationship of mediating variables to MD

(I) Job-related processes contributing to MD	(II) Mediating organizational variables		
	Authority paths and decision processes	Information flow and information systems	Individual and organizational relationships
Staffing processes (Job placement)	1. Recommendations of other managers and peers influence selection of individual. 2. Manager makes decision the individual can respect. 3. Promotion within Dept/ functional speciality. 4. Complex system control records.	1. Manager uses Personnel Department candidates, identification system. 2. Outside information about openings closed to individuals and group. 3. Well designed system including procedures, data processing, etc. 4. Group aware of unit openings.	1. Individual can express point of view but not change decision. 2. Best-liked person in group gets job. 3. Low trust in objectivity of selection decisions. 4. Long-service persons move ahead. 5. Individual counseled by group and Personnel.
Goal-setting processes (Defining expected results)	1. Quotas, production and performance standards. 2. Third party recommends; group can influence (mutual goal-setting). 3. May be serial or small total goals. 4. Regularly adjusted.	1. Broad goals set at top; individuals, units, and managers design and set unit and individual goals. 2. Upward feedback involves progress reviews and evaluation of units. 3. Well developed formal planning system around financial controls.	1. Individual goals considered but may still be in conflict with organization. 2. High commitment to group goals but not necessarily company goals. 3. Group goal interdependency understood, but not group to total organization. 4. Group cooperation in setting group goals.
Work performance (How work is done)	1. Specific "how to" job descriptions. 2. Group can make changes subject to higher authority's OK. 3. Serial or small total task accomplishment.	1. Group information shared with those accountable for results. 2. Sharing of ideas within group. 3. Well developed control system at unit level as well as top.	1. Intragroup conflict dealt with, intergroup conflict suppressed. 2. Intergroup cooperation high. 3. Individuals feel responsible for each other within group.
Evaluation processes (How work results are evaluated)	1. Peer evaluation/total group evaluation. 2. Formal group, peer and individual evaluation (all, combination, or one). 3. Feedback to group.	1. Direct feedback to groups on unit results. 2. Group and job-oriented appraisal with some personality measures (standards of performance). 3. Usually formalized.	1. Peer evaluation (in group) generally agrees with individual evaluation. 2. Fairly high trust level and loyalty in group. 3. Excuses, blaming, and low ownership in work performed by outside groups.
MD practices Programs, systems, procedures suitable to I and II above	1. Manager and (usually) groups decide on training. 2. Formal (off work) in-company and sometimes outside programs. 3. Formal policies and procedures. 4. Individual goes along with group.	1. Group information shared within group. 2. Information outside of unit not generally available. 3. Formal information movement to span group. 4. Officials meet with groups and units to share information.	1. Groups learn how to problem-solve. 2. Group dynamics tough and understood. 3. Participating leadership style tough. 4. Interdepartment relationships defined, intragroup relationships loosely defined.
Behavior outputs Behavior to be expected from individual	1. Respond in predicted way. 2. Follow group norms. 3. Rely on group for needed know-how. 4. Adapt only at group rate of change.	1. Share ideas and suggestions where it will be seen to benefit total group. 2. Search for organizational information through informal channels. 3. Distort organizational information.	1. Confront intragroup conflict. 2. Help group solve problems. 3. Commit self to solve department problems. 4. Be rejected by group if incompatible (moderate mobility).

Coordinative organizational structure: relationship of mediating variables to MD

(I) Job-related processes contributing to MD	(II) Mediating organizational variables		
	Authority paths and decision processes	Information flow and information systems	Individual and organizational relationships
Staffing processes (Job placement)	1. Individual recommends self. 2. Manager makes decision to accept. 3. Promotion to other departments and functional areas. 4. Broad policies, simple procedures.	1. Manager informs Personnel, who post job information. 2. Individual receives job information on all jobs in organization. 3. Well designed information system. 4. Individual applies directly for job, can request information directly.	1. Individual goals are primary in job selection, resulting in low conflict/high cooperation. 2. Most competent person gets job. 3. High trust in selection decisions. 4. Loyalty/length of service not primary decision. 5. Counseling available from numerous sources.
Goal-setting processes (Defining expected results)	1. Expected results-coordinated deadlines. 2. Individuals I.D. and set own goals coordinated with others. 3. Specific goals based on individual expertise. 4. Highly flexible.	1. Goal-setting process initiated by individuals and collected into unit and organizational goals. 2. Interunit sharing of information for coordination purposes. 3. Informal and broadly defined planning system.	1. Individual goals are primary, they combine to form group and organization goals. 2. High commitment to individual, group, and organization goals. 3. Interdependency of individual department and organization goals is understood in individual's field. 4. High degree of goal collaboration.
Work performance (How work is done)	1. Broad key areas of responsibility. Individual decides specifics. 2. Individual makes changes within broad limits: i.e., relates to others' goals. 3. Total task accomplishment based on expertise.	1. Individual shares information with those who need it. 2. Individual offers ideas where appropriate. 3. Full use of latest communication ideas to facilitate information flow.	1. Conflict throughout organization openly confronted and resolved. 2. High level of cooperation between individual and groups in specific fields of technology. 3. Feeling of responsibility to others for individual contributions.
Evaluation processes (How work results are evaluated)	1. Individuals evaluate selves against goals. 2. Broad general policy, not formal (MBO type). 3. Feedback to individual.	1. Self evaluation based on goal achievement. 2. Results measured against preset goals, not personality. 3. Formalized system of goal definition, no formal appraisal system	1. No conflict in evaluation because individual evaluates self against preset goals. 2. High level of trust. 3. Low level of excuses, blaming, and shifting of ownership to others.

(I) Job-related processes contributing to MD	(II) Mediating organizational variables		
	Authority paths and decision processes	Information flow and information systems	Individual and organizational relationships
MD practices Programs, systems, procedures suitable to I and II above	1. Individual decides own training. 2. Informal, experience-based, experimental. 3. Loosely structured policies. 4. Individual may use manager and groups as resource and help.	1. Nonformal system open and multiple file of information throughout organization. 2. All communication systems geared to provide all information desired by individual. 3. Opportunity to test utility of information. 4. Formal information management meetings not needed.	1. Team-building and confrontation is practiced. 2. Use of T groups. 3. Notion of leadership rests with competency as followed. 4. Loosely defined relationships.
Behavior outputs Behavior to be expected from individual	1. Have unpredictable responses—response will accomplish goals. 2. Not be concerned about rules and norms. 3. Search for answers to situation. 4. Adjust to situation.	1. Move freely within organization—going over or around boss is common and accepted. 2. Share ideas and suggestions. 3. Have little or no need for information through informed sources. 4. Give a minimum of distortion.	1. Bring conflict out in open. 2. Value conflict resolution (all types, levels, etc.). 3. Maintain helping relationship (one helps another). 4. Leave as technology dictates (high mobility).

Index